Meredith Levy   Noel Goodey   Diana Goodey

Messages

Workbook

3

My name is ....

I am in Class ....

The name of my school is ....

My English teacher is ....

My address is ....

....

....

Date ....

CAMBRIDGE
UNIVERSITY PRESS

1 Connections

STEP 1

1 Questions: meeting new people G→ 1a, 2a

Danny and Marek are in Barcelona. Write Danny's questions.

DANNY: speak / English?

¹ *Do you speak English?*

MAREK: Yes, I do.

DANNY: What / your name?

2 _____

MAREK: Marek Kotarski.

DANNY: live / in Spain?

3 _____

MAREK: No, I don't.

DANNY: Where / come from?

4 _____

MAREK: Poland.

DANNY: What / do in Spain?

5 _____

MAREK: I'm on a school trip.

DANNY: stay / at the hostel?

6 _____

MAREK: Yes, I am.

DANNY: What / think of Barcelona?

7 _____

MAREK: It's great! I really like it.

2 Questions: short answers G→ 1a, 2a

Look at the pictures of Ruth and her brothers. Complete the questions and write short answers.

1 *Does* _____ Ruth live in a house?

No, she doesn't. _____

2 _____ she got a very large bedroom?

_____

3 _____ there any posters on the wall?

_____

4 _____ Ruth play a musical instrument?

_____

5 _____ she using her computer now?

_____

6 _____ Ruth's brothers younger than her?

_____

7 _____ the boys share a bedroom?

_____

8 _____ they got a computer?

_____

3 Making questions

Someone is asking you some questions. These are true answers for you. What are the questions?

1 _Are you a student?_
Yes, I am.

2 _____
Yes, I do.

3 _____
No, she doesn't.

4 _____
Yes, they have.

5 _____
No, he isn't.

6 _____
No, I don't.

4 Key expressions

Greetings and introductions

Read the information and write the conversations.

A Luke and Jack are waiting at the bus stop.
Tina, Luke's friend, is coming towards them.

1 Tina greets Luke and asks how he is.
2 Luke answers that he's fine.
3 Then he introduces Tina to Jack.
4 Jack greets Tina.

TINA: ¹ _Hi, Luke. How_ _____ ?

LUKE: ² _____

   ³ _____

JACK: ⁴ _____

B Caroline Pitt is a student. Her mother
is visiting the school for the first time.

1 Caroline introduces her mother to her
science teacher, Mr Gray.
2 Mrs Pitt greets Mr Gray.
3 Mr Gray greets Mrs Pitt.

CAROLINE: ¹ _____

MRS PITT: ² _____

MR GRAY: ³ _____

5 Listening *At Natalie's party*

Read the questions. Then listen to the conversation at Natalie's party and tick (✓) *Yes* or *No*.

		Yes	No
1	Are Adam and Kelly friends?		✓
2	Does Adam live in London?		
3	Has he got a job?		
4	Is he staying with relatives?		
5	Does Kelly come from England?		
6	Does her family live in London?		
7	Does she often see Natalie at school?		

6 Extension *A new friend*

Imagine you're writing your first letter to a new pen friend. Think of at least three questions that you'd like to ask.

What's your favourite subject at school?
Do you like skateboarding?

_____

_____

_____

_____

_____

_____

_____

1 Key vocabulary *Countries and nationalities*

Can you complete these sentences with the right information? Use words for countries and nationalities.

1 Veracruz is a city in M*exico* _____ .

2 The capital of J_____ is Tokyo.

3 The F_____ word for 'thank you' is *merci*.

4 Ian Thorpe comes from Sydney. He's a great

   A_____ swimmer.

5 Krakow and Gdansk are cities in P_____ .

6 There are 50 stars on the A_____ flag.

7 Federico Fellini was a great film director. He was

   I_____ .

8 C_____ is the country to the north of the

   USA.

9 *Paella* is a very popular S_____ dish. You

   make it with rice, chicken and fish.

10 Diego Maradona was a brilliant footballer. He played for

   A_____ .

3 Present simple G ▶ 1a

Write the sentences in a different way. Use verbs in the present simple.

1 Andreas is Greek.

   Andreas _*comes*_ from Greece.

2 His home is on a small island.

   He _____ on a small island.

3 His mother and father have both got jobs in the local hotel.

   His parents both _____ in the local hotel.

4 The island hasn't got a school, so a boat takes the boys to school every day.

   There _____ a school on the island, so the

   boys _____ to school by boat every day.

5 Andreas isn't a football player, but he thinks swimming is great.

   Andreas _____ football,

   but he _____ swimming.

2 Reading *A puzzle: what's her name?*

Read the information in the puzzle and write ✓ or ✗ in the table. Then write the name of the girl in the photo.

puzzle page Who's the girl in the photo?

- ✪ Louise is very good at drawing and she loves painting.
- ✪ Alice and her family have got a flat in Paris.
- ✪ Christine walks along the river every day when she goes to school.
- ✪ Alice and Christine aren't in the same class, but they live in the same street.
- ✪ Louise doesn't really enjoy living in Paris. She often stays in her grandparents' village at the weekend.
- ✪ Alice's father takes her to school in the car. She's studying art, but she isn't very interested in it.
- ✪ Louise meets Christine at about eight fifteen in the morning and they go to school together.
- ✪ Christine wants to be an art teacher when she leaves school.
- ✪ Alice and Christine usually share a table in the school canteen at lunchtime.
- ✪ Louise's family have lunch together at home.

My name's _____ and I live in Paris. I always walk to school and I come home for lunch. My favourite subject is art.

	lives in Paris	walks to school	has lunch at home	likes art
Alice				
Louise				✓
Christine				

4 Present continuous G▶ 2a

Find six differences between the two pictures. Write sentences with the present continuous.

A   B

Peter   Helen   Peter   Helen

Rebecca   Rebecca

In A Peter and Helen are wearing sweaters, but in B they're wearing T-shirts.

5 Present continuous and present simple G▶ 1b, 2b, 2c

Complete the sentences about picture A in Exercise 4.
Use the present continuous or the present simple form of the verbs in the box.

beat	play	look	feel	~~sit~~	want	not watch	not win	not like

Peter and his two sisters ¹ *are sitting* at the table. He and Helen ² _____

a game of chess. Peter is older than Helen and he usually ³ _____ her at chess.

But today he ⁴ _____ and Helen ⁵ _____ pleased.

Rebecca ⁶ _____ their game. She ⁷ _____ chess. She's much

more interested in her magazine. She ⁸ _____ to join the Photography Club

at school and she ⁹ _____ for information about the best digital cameras for sale.

6 Extension *People I know*

In your notebook, write sentences about people you know. Use the present simple and the present continuous.

My sister is brilliant at drawing. My uncle teaches maths at the university.
My friend Carla is learning to play the drums.

'English Worldwide!': Vocabulary check

1 Look at the words in the box. Can you find two nouns?

Nouns: _____ _____

> technology   worldwide   like   connect
> French-speaking   over   communicate
> each other   Earth   ~~alone~~

2 Complete the sentences. Use the words in the box in Exercise 1.

1 There wasn't anyone in the room with me.

I was _____*alone*_____ .

2 There was a Russian player and a Spanish player in the tennis final. They spoke to _____ _____ in English.

3 In Canada not everyone speaks English. There are seven million _____ Canadians.

4 A: I think there are about 140 countries in the world.

B: No, there are _____ 140. There are at least 190.

5 'On _____' means the same as 'on this planet'.

6 The mobile phone and the digital camera are examples of modern _____ .

7 The Internet can _____ you with people all over the world.

8 My grandfather was amazing. He loved animals and he could _____ with them.

9 A: What does _____ mean?

B: It means 'all over the world'.

10 Big cities _____ London, New York, Rome and Barcelona are always full of tourists.

3 Translate these sentences into your language.

1 A: What are you doing?
B: I'm trying to open this carton of orange juice.

----

2 A: Where does Luigi live?
B: He lives in Bologna.

----

3 A: Is Montreal in Canada?
B: Yes, it is. It's a French-speaking city.

----

4 A: Do people in Britain have hot chocolate for breakfast?
B: I don't know.

----

5 My aunt speaks Spanish and Italian, and she's learning Greek at the moment.

----

6 A: You aren't playing very well. 150 isn't a very good score.
B: I know. I don't often play computer games.

Unit 1 Learning diary

Date _____

Now I know how to:

	Easy	Not bad	Difficult

- introduce people and greet people. ☐ ☐ ☐

  This is _____ . She's in my class at school.

  Hello. Nice to _____ .

  Hi, Jack. How _____ ? How do _____ , Mr Grant?

- ask questions when I meet new people. ☐ ☐ ☐

  Where _____ from? I'm from England.

  What are you _____ here? I'm on holiday.

- give my nationality and say where I come from. ☐ ☐ ☐

  I'm _____ . I'm from _____ .

- talk about my daily life. ☐ ☐ ☐

  I get up at _____ .

  I _____ for breakfast.

  I don't _____ .

- talk about things that are happening now. ☐ ☐ ☐

  I'm sitting _____ and I'm _____ .

- write a report about my class. ☐ ☐ ☐

KEY WORDS

Countries	Nationalities
Mexico	Mexican
Greece	

WORD WORK

Numbers

1¼	One and a quarter
2½	
8·95	
65%	
100	
700	
18,000	
3,000,000	

2 Past events

1 Past simple verbs (G) 3a

Complete the crossword with the past simple form of the verbs.

		¹				²	
³		⁴A	R	G	U	E	D
							⁵
⁶			⁷				
		⁸					
⁹							
	¹⁰		¹¹				
¹²	¹³						
	¹⁴						
¹⁵							

Across

4 ~~argue~~
6 buy
8 run
9 go
10 leave
12 see
14 sell
15 break

Down

1 catch
2 begin
3 write
5 stop
7 try
9 is
11 take
13 are

3 Past simple: questions (G) 3a

Look at the answers and complete the questions. Use the verbs in the box.

| get | do | go rollerblading | ~~leave~~ | arrive | go | meet |

1 _What time_ did Sonia _leave_ home?
   At quarter to ten.

2 _____ she _____ Jill?
   Outside the post office.

3 _____ they _____ ?
   To the park.

4 _____ they _____ to the park?
   By bus.

5 _____ they _____ ?
   At about ten thirty.

6 _____ Sonia _____ at the park?
   She went rollerblading.

7 _____ Jill _____ too?
   No, she didn't. She sat and watched the birds.

2 Past simple: negative (G) 3a

Complete the sentences. Use verbs from the crossword in the negative form.

1 I can't find Kerry's phone number. I _didn't write_ it in my address book.

2 Franca couldn't get any postcards. They _____ them at the village shop.

3 My shorts and trainers were in my bag, but I _____ my tennis racket with me.

4 Dad _____ to the market, so there _____ much food in the house yesterday.

5 We _____ Tom this morning. He _____ the 8.15 train. He probably walked to school.

6 I saw some cheap trainers in the shoe shop, but I _____ them. They _____ very nice.

4 Listening *Five conversations*

Listen to the conversations. Tick (✓) the right answer: A, B or C.

1 Where did Sam and Martina meet?

A ☐   B ✓   C ☐

2 Where did Tim catch the bus?

A ☐   B ☐   C ☐

3 What time did Julie leave school?

A ☐   B ☐   C ☐

4 Who had a phone conversation with Sophie last night?

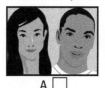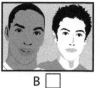

A ☐   B ☐   C ☐

5 Where did Tony stay?

A ☐   B ☐   C ☐

5 Key expressions *Apologies*

Complete the conversations. Use two words from the box for each answer.

Don't	fault	all	worry	doesn't	~~sorry~~	your	matter	~~I'm~~	right

A ANA: I think you've got my umbrella.

GIRL: Oh, really? ¹ _I'm sorry._ I thought it was mine.

ANA: That's ² _____ _____ . ³ _____ _____ about it.

B MRS SAYER: Didn't you get any vegetables? I asked you to go to the shop on your way home.

JAY: Yes, I know, but it wasn't open.

MRS SAYER: Oh, I see.

JAY: I'm sorry.

MRS SAYER: It ⁴ _____ _____ . It isn't ⁵ _____ _____ .

6 Extension *Events in your life*

In your notebook, draw a time line and write some important dates in your life.
Then write sentences about what happened.

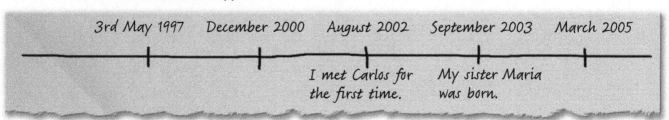

3rd May 1997   December 2000   August 2002   September 2003   March 2005

I met Carlos for the first time.   My sister Maria was born.

Key vocabulary *Verbs describing actions*

Write the verbs. Then write the past simple form.

		Verb	Past simple
1	Boats, ships and ferries do this.	*sail*	*sailed*
2	Planes do this when they arrive at an airport.	l_____	_____
3	If you drop things, they do this.	f_____	_____
4	Cars often do this when they're in an accident.	c_____	_____
5	Kangaroos and frogs can do this.	j_____	_____
6	If you throw stones into a river, they do this.	s_____	_____
7	Tennis players do this to the tennis ball.	h_____	_____
8	Birds can do this, but people can't.	f_____	_____

2 Past continuous and past simple Ⓖ⟶ 3b, 4b, 4c

Nadia and Patrick are talking about the first time they met.
Complete their sentences. Use the past continuous or the past simple.

NADIA: I ¹ *met* (meet) Patrick when I

² *was going* (go) to school with my friend

Janet. We were on our bikes and it was a really

windy morning. We ³ _____ (ride) along

Stone Street when a dog ran in front of me. I

⁴ _____ (not go) very fast, but I

⁵ _____ (fall) off my bike. My things flew

all over the street. It was awful, but it was funny too.

Then Patrick ⁶ _____ (arrive).

PATRICK: Yes, I ⁷ _____ (come) round the

corner when I ⁸ _____ (find) these

two crazy girls in front of me. Bits of paper

⁹ _____ (fly) everywhere and they

¹⁰ _____ (try) to catch them. When I

first ¹¹ _____ (see) Nadia, she

¹² _____ (dance) in the wind and she

¹³ _____ (laugh). I think that's

when I fell in love with her.

3 Past continuous and past simple: questions and answers Ⓖ 3a. 4a

Look at the text in Exercise 2 and complete the questions and answers.

1 What __was__ Nadia doing when she __met__ Patrick?

She __was going to school.__

2 _____ Nadia going to school on her own?

No, she _____ .

3 _____ Nadia and Janet riding their bikes?

_____ , they _____ .

4 What happened when they _____ riding along Stone Street?

A dog _____ in front of Nadia.

5 Did Nadia _____ off her bike?

_____ , she _____ .

6 What _____ Patrick doing when he saw the girls?

He _____ round the corner.

7 What _____ the two girls doing?

They _____ to catch the pieces of paper.

8 _____ Nadia crying?

_____ , she _____ . She _____ .

4 Reading *The night the* Titanic *sank*

Read the text about the *Titanic*. Then find words in the text that match these descriptions.

1 A city in the south of England.   _____
2 Two words that mean 'not very many'.   _____
3 People on a ship, a train, a bus or
  a plane.   _____
4 A person who works on a ship.   _____
5 A word that means 'didn't die'.   _____
6 Another word for 'sea'.   _____

On 14th April 1912, the *Titanic* was sailing across the Atlantic. It was the largest and most expensive ship of its time and it was carrying 2,228 people on its first journey, from Southampton in England to New York.

The night was very cold. At 11.40, a few passengers were talking and playing cards, but most people were getting ready for bed or were already asleep. High up in the 'crow's nest', the young sailor Frederick Fleet was watching the sea. It was quiet and the stars were shining. Then Frederick saw something. Immediately he picked up the phone and shouted: 'Iceberg ahead!'

The *Titanic* changed direction, but it was sailing fast. The ship was still turning when it hit the iceberg and a long hole opened along its side, deep under the water. Water started to come into the bottom of the ship. The *Titanic* was sinking.

Frederick Fleet was one of the 705 people who survived. He was watching from a small lifeboat when the *Titanic* broke in two and sank to the bottom of the ocean.

5 Extension *Time to talk*

a Alan is having a conversation with a friend. Read what he says.

ALAN:
- Hi! How are you?
- I tried to find you at lunchtime yesterday. Where were you?
- Oh, right. So what did you have for lunch?
- Were you on your own?
- And what did you do after lunch?
- Yes, I see. Well, I must go. I'll see you later, OK?

🔊 Now listen to the conversation.

b Read Alan's sentences again. Then imagine he's talking to you. Think about the answers you want to make.

c 🔊 Close your book, listen to the sentences and respond.

'Survival!': Vocabulary check

1 Look at the words in the box. Can you find four verbs?

Verbs: ....

below	survive	branch	grass	heart attack
knife	over	fall asleep	passenger	shake
~~rabbit~~	surface	cut	noise	

2 Match the words in the box in Exercise 1 with these sentences.

1 This animal has got long ears.   .... *rabbit* ....

2 You need this when you eat steak.   ....

3 You do this when you're very tired.   ....

4 If you have this, you become ill very suddenly.   ....

5 This word is the opposite of *above*.   ....

6 You can't do this on the moon. There isn't any air or water.   ....

7 Cows eat this.   ....

8 If you're very scared, you sometimes do this.   ....

9 It's sometimes scary when you hear this during the night.   ....

10 If you do this to your finger, it hurts.   ....

11 When you swim in the sea, you can't stay under this for a long time. ....

12 This person is in the car but isn't driving it.   ....

13 This is a part of a tree.   ....

14 This word can mean *finished*.   ....

3 Translate these sentences into your language.

1 When I was in England, I went to London, but I didn't go to Buckingham Palace.

....

....

2 A: Where were you last night? I phoned you, but you weren't at home.
  B: I was having a shower when you called.

....

....

....

3 A: Did you see the film on TV yesterday?
  B: No, I didn't. I was doing my homework.

....

....

....

4 I didn't enjoy that book. I fell asleep when I was reading it.

....

....

5 A: I'm sorry. I wasn't listening. What did you say?
  B: Don't worry about it. It wasn't important.

....

....

....

6 A: Did you hear that noise?
  B: Yes, I did. What was it?

....

....

....

Unit 2 Learning diary

Date _____

Now I know how to:

	Easy	Not bad	Difficult

● apologise. ☐ ☐ ☐

I'm _____ . _____ my fault.

● accept an apology. ☐ ☐ ☐

Don't _____ about it. _____ all right. It _____ matter.

● talk about events in the past. ☐ ☐ ☐

I went to _____ yesterday. I didn't _____ last night.

What did _____ ? I stayed at home.

● form the simple past of regular and irregular verbs. ☐ ☐ ☐

wait	*waited*	live	_____	see	_____	decide	_____
come	*came*	go	_____	buy	_____	leave	_____
listen	_____	finish	_____	explain	_____	be	_____
get	_____	sit	_____	watch	_____	fall	_____

● talk about actions in progress in the past. ☐ ☐ ☐

At 8 o'clock this morning, it _____ raining.

At 8 o'clock this morning, I _____ .

● talk about interrupted actions in the past. ☐ ☐ ☐

The Titanic _____ across the Atlantic when it _____ .

● write a short story. ☐ ☐ ☐

KEY WORDS

Action verbs

land = _____ *(in my language)*

jump = _____   hit = _____

fly = _____   sail = _____

fall = _____   sink = _____

WORD WORK

Link words

and _____   _____

_____   _____

_____   _____

3 People

1 Adjectives

Put the letters in order and make adjectives. Write them under the pictures.

dol   tafs   lalt
ryluc   ~~glon~~   goyun
thros   yinflerd

1 *long* _____ 2 _____ 3 _____ 4 _____

5 _____ 6 _____ 7 _____ 8 _____

2 Comparatives and superlatives: regular forms (G) 25a, 25b, 25c

Complete the sentences. Use the comparative or superlative form of the adjectives in the box.

big   expensive   popular   busy   young   ~~tall~~   heavy   ~~dark~~

1 Paolo is *the tallest* _____ member of our team. He's more than two metres tall.

2 My sister's hair is *darker than* _____ mine. Hers is nearly black.

3 Jay is nearly 18. He's a bit _____ Ana.

4 Everyone loves Elena. She's one of _____ students in the school.

5 Asia is 44,000 km², so it's _____ Africa. It's the largest continent in the world.

6 The world's largest dinosaurs weighed more than 100 tons. One of these animals was _____ ten elephants.

7 It isn't cheap to live in Tokyo. It's one of _____ cities in the world.

8 Cumberland Road is _____ street in our town. It's always full of traffic.

3 Comparatives and superlatives: regular and irregular forms (G) 25d

Look at the exam results and complete the sentences. Write one word in each space.

Diane Turner		Steve McDonald	
Maths	53%	Maths	71%
Science	57%	Science	60%
History	65%	History	58%
Spanish	83%	Information technology	81%
English	78%	English	48%
French	98%	Art	66%
Art	60%	Music	79%

Diane's result in the French exam was the ¹ *best* in the class. She finds languages easier and ² _____ interesting ³ _____ her other subjects, but she passed all her exams. Her ⁴ _____ subject is maths. Steve's maths and science results were ⁵ _____ than Diane's, but his history result was ⁶ _____ than hers. English is the ⁷ _____ difficult subject for Steve. His ⁸ _____ subjects are music and information technology.

4 Reading *Veracruz*

Read Ana's description of her city, Veracruz. Then read the sentences and write *T* (true), *F* (false) or *?* (the answer isn't in the text).

Veracruz is in the south of Mexico, about 440 km east of the capital, Mexico City. It's the country's oldest sea port and I love watching the ships that come in from all over the world.

It's very different from London. It's a much smaller city. There are only about 555,000 people in Veracruz. In London there are over seven million — it's got the highest population of all European cities. I sometimes feel lonely in London. There are people everywhere, but it isn't easy to make friends.

Veracruz is also a warmer, sunnier city than London. Everyone sits outside at café tables and there's usually the sound of music — salsa bands, traditional guitars or marimba bands with their metal drums. At night there's dancing in the city squares. People say it's the happiest and most musical city in Mexico.

The food is fabulous too, especially the seafood. Our most famous dish is fish in hot tomato sauce, and you can get wonderful milkshakes and ice creams. The most popular café is the Gran Café del Portal, which serves the best coffee in town.

Of course there's nice food and great music in London too, but everything's more expensive than in Veracruz. And the weather is a lot worse!

1 Veracruz and London are both capital cities. _F_

2 You can often see foreign ships in Veracruz. ....

3 Veracruz is a larger city than London. ....

4 There are more people in London than in other European cities. ....

5 Ana has got some English friends in Veracruz. ....

6 You can sometimes hear marimba bands in London. ....

7 Prices are higher in Veracruz than in London. ....

8 Veracruz has got a better climate than London. ....

5 Extension *Hidden adjectives*

Find the hidden adjectives in these sentences. There are comparative and superlative forms. Write them in the lists.

1 Buy yourself a stereo!

2 Don't be stupid!

3 When ice starts to melt, it forms water.

4 Our friends from Oslo were staying here.

5 Is your uncle a nervous man?

6 Carol destroyed her brother's computer game.

7 Ring me tomorrow or send an email.

8 If you're tired, have a siesta.

Comparative	Superlative
faster	....
....	....
....	....
....	....

1 Key vocabulary *Personality*

a Choose the best adjective for each picture.

> confident   clever   adventurous
> ~~independent~~   easy-going   shy   lazy
> moody   generous   hard-working

1 *independent*   2 _____

3 _____   4 _____

5 _____   6 _____

7 _____   8 _____

9 _____   10 _____

b These sentences aren't right! Replace the underlined words with different adjectives from 1a.

1 You need to be ~~clever~~ if you want to try mountain climbing. ___adventurous___

2 Actors are shy in front of the cameras.

_____

3 Lazy people are ready to work ten hours a day.

_____

4 Independent people enjoy sharing things with other people. _____

5 Easy-going people often get unhappy or angry. Their feelings change quickly. _____

2 as ... as Ⓖ➤ 26

Write the sentences in a different way.
Use *(not) as ... as.*

1 Jane is more confident than Sarah.

Sarah *isn't as confident as* _____ Jane.

2 Alan is lazier than George.

George _____ Alan.

3 Jack and I are both 178 cm tall.

I _____ Jack.

4 A giraffe has got very long legs. A zebra's legs are shorter.

A zebra's legs _____
a giraffe's.

5 Olga isn't better than me at maths. We're about the same.

I _____ Olga at maths.

6 My mother's got very dark hair and mine is the same colour.

My hair _____ my mother's.

7 I think your idea is better than Matt's.

I don't think Matt's idea _____
yours.

8 The lasagne wasn't very nice, but the pizza was worse.

The lasagne _____ the pizza.

3 Key expressions *Asking for a description* (G) → 20a, 20b

Complete the conversation. Choose the right sentences from the list (a–j).

A: I went to Dave's place on Sunday. I met his new girlfriend.

B: Oh! ¹ _e_ ?

A: I think she's nice. ² _____

B: ³ _____ ?

A: She's tall and fair. ⁴ _____

B: Oh, right.

A: Dave's sister Nicole was there too. Her son's six months old now.

B: ⁵ _____ ?

A: He's beautiful. ⁶ _____ He's got a round face and a lovely smile.

B: ⁷ _____ ?

A: Yes, he does. ⁸ _____

a What does she look like?
b Does she like you?
c His hair's black.
d They've got the same eyes and mouth.
e ~~What's she like?~~
f What does he look like?
g She's got blue eyes and short curly hair.
h I don't like him.
i She's very friendly and easy-going.
j Does he look like Nicole?

4 Listening *Leo's friends*

a 🔊 Listen to Leo describing three of his friends. Match their names with the people in the picture (A–E).

Harry _____   Erica _____   Simon _____

b 🔊 Listen again and tick (✓) the right answer: a, b or c.

1 Harry is   a Leo's brother.   ☐   3 Erica is   a confident.   ☐
              b very intelligent.   ☐   b moody.   ☐
              c cleverer than Erica.   ☐   c shy.   ☐

2 Harry isn't   a as tall as Leo.   ☐   4 Simon is   a funny.   ☐
              b as young as Erica.   ☐   b kind.   ☐
              c as nice as Simon.   ☐   c generous.   ☐

5 Extension *A description*

Choose one of Leo's other friends in the picture in Exercise 4. Think of
a name for him/her and write a short description in your notebook.

'Daniel Trent's web page': Vocabulary check

1 Underline the right word in each sentence.

1   Luigi's (*tidy* / *cool* / *embarrassing*). He always wears modern clothes and listens to the most modern music.

2   This is my homepage. (*Contact* / *Click* / *Go*) on the links at the bottom of the page and you'll find details about my interests.

3   It (*puts* / *goes* / *takes*) about an hour to get to London from here.

4   I live in Grange Street. There's a sports centre (*nearby* / *25 km away* / *next*), so I walk there every morning.

5   Do you want my email address so that you can (*connect* / *contact* / *communicate*) me?

6   The living room is (*comfortable* / *untidy* / *good-looking*). There are books and magazines all over the floor.

7   When I got to school yesterday I found that there was a big hole in my trousers. It was really (*small* / *embarrassing* / *nice*).

8   Zoe's very funny. She knows a lot of good (*cafés* / *books* / *jokes*).

9   Gary's the (*player* / *captain* / *winner*) of his local football team. He's a good leader.

10 My brother broke my DVD player last week. I was very (*annoyed* / *unpopular* / *lucky*).

11 Kirsty's a very (*untidy* / *easy-going* / *tidy*) person. She cleans her room every week.

12 I go out every Saturday night with my friends. It's great. We always have a lot of (*problems* / *tickets* / *fun*).

2 Translate these sentences into your language.

1   A: What does Tina's boyfriend look like?
    B: He's quite short. He isn't as tall as Tina. He's very good-looking.

    ----

2   A: What's your new guitar teacher like?
    B: He's better than my last teacher. He's more easy-going.

    ----

3   Oh, you've got some new trainers. Look! They're the same as mine!

    ----

4   A: Can you show me the cheapest DVD player, please?
    B: This is the cheapest, but it isn't as good as the others.

    ----

5   A: I look awful in my school photo.
    B: Well, mine is worse than yours. I look like an alien!

    ----

6   I don't want to play chess. I think it's the most boring game in the world.

Unit 3 Learning diary

Date _____

Now I know how to:

	Easy	Not bad	Difficult
compare and describe two things.	☐	☐	☐

_____ is easier than _____ .

_____ is more _____ than _____ .

My _____ than _____ .

	Easy	Not bad	Difficult
compare one thing with more than one other thing.	☐	☐	☐

_____ is my most difficult school subject.

Mount Everest is the _____ in the world.

_____ is _____ in the world.

	Easy	Not bad	Difficult
talk about differences and similarities.	☐	☐	☐

My _____ is as tall as me.

I'm not as _____ as _____ .

	Easy	Not bad	Difficult
ask about someone's appearance or personality.	☐	☐	☐

What _____ look like?   He's got fair hair.

What _____ like?   She's very friendly.

Does Ana _____ her brother? Yes, they've got the same colour eyes.

	Easy	Not bad	Difficult
write a web page about myself.	☐	☐	☐

KEY WORDS
Personality adjectives

hard-working _____   _____

_____   _____

_____   _____

_____   _____

WORD WORK
Opposites

shy   confident _____

easy-going _____

unfriendly _____

stupid _____

untidy _____

popular _____

hard-working _____

4 Places

1 Key vocabulary *Places and buildings*

Look at the pictures and write the words in the puzzle.

					7						
			1	S	T	A	D	I	U	M	

2

3

4

5

6

(1)

(2)

(3)

(4)

(5)

(6)

(7)

2 Activities

Match the verbs with the nouns.

1 visit   a concert
2 go   b some new clothes
3 take   c lunch
4 look round   d cinema
5 have   e a boat trip
6 go to a   f my friends
7 buy   g the shops
8 go to the   h swimming

1 *f*   5 ....
2 ....   6 ....
3 ....   7 ....
4 ....   8 ....

3 Suggestions Ⓖ➔ 22a, 22b

Complete the suggestions. Use places and activities from Exercises 1 and 2.

1 Dave wants to see a film.

   DAVE: Why *don't we go to* *the cinema* ?

2 Judith would like to go down the river in a boat.

   JUDITH: Let's ....

3 It's lunchtime and Annie wants to try the Dolphin Café.

   ANNIE: Shall .... ?

4 Paul knows there's a good exhibition at the art gallery.

   PAUL: How about .... ?

5 Rob wants to spend some time in the shopping centre.

   ROB: Let's .... the shops.

6 Ilse would like to see the castle.

   ILSE: Why .... ?

4 Key expressions *Making and responding to suggestions*

Look at the pictures and complete the conversations.

ELISE: How about [1] *going on the river?*

CATHY: [2] _____ idea. Let's go!

PETRA: Where [3] _____ ? To the castle

or the mosque?

MARK: Which do you prefer?

PETRA: I [4] _____ . They're both

interesting.

MARK: Well, I think I'd [5] _____

_____ .

PETRA: OK. [6] _____ with me.

5 Listening *What shall we do?*

🔊 Rosa and Luke are making an arrangement for tomorrow. Listen to their phone conversation and write the information in the box.

Place:	National [1] *Gallery* in Trafalgar [2] _____
Price:	[3] _____
Opening hours:	[4] _____ to [5] _____
Meeting place:	Pizza [6] _____ in [7] _____ Street
Meeting time:	[8] _____

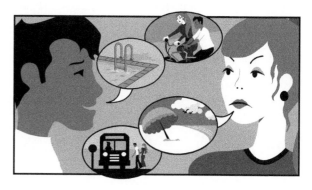

SANDRO: Shall [7] _____ ?

ALICE: No, I [8] _____ do that.

Why [9] _____ ?

SANDRO: All [10] _____ . Shall we

go on our bikes?

ALICE: No, let's [11] _____ .

6 Extension *My ideal street*

Look at the example. In your notebook, make a map of your ideal street. Draw your home on the map, then draw and label the places you would like to have around you.

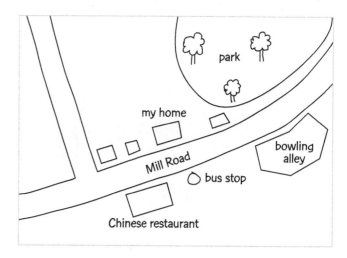

1 much, many and a lot of (G) 23a, 23b

Complete the sentences. Use *much, many* or *a lot of*.

1 My grandfather puts _a lot of_ sugar in his tea.

2 Our library hasn't got _____ interesting books.

3 You can find _____ useful information on the Internet.

4 Ana hasn't got _____ friends in London.

5 There isn't _____ water in the lake at the moment.

6 Do you know _____ Beatles songs?

7 They show _____ good films at the Rex Cinema.

8 How _____ money have we got?

2 too much / many, enough (G) 24a, 24b

Look at the pictures and complete the sentences. Use *too much, too many* or *enough*.

1 I haven't got _enough_ meat. There's _____ salad.

2 There are _____ girls here. There aren't _____ boys.

3 He does _____ work. He doesn't get _____ sleep.

4 I haven't got _____ coffee. There are _____ people here.

5 A: The film starts at eight. Have we got _____ time?

   B: No! There's _____ traffic.

6 A: There are always _____ passengers on this train.

   B: That's because there aren't _____ trains.

3 Reading *Sports in the outback*

Read the text about two sports in Alice Springs. Then read the sentences and circle the right answer: a, b or c.

Goat races are popular at Lightning Ridge. But in Alice Springs, another town in the Australian outback, people haven't got much time for goats. They're busy organising two other unusual sports.

In May there's camel racing. This started in 1971, when two friends decided to have a race on camels along the dry bed of the Todd River. Now the Camel Cup is a very big race and a lot of people come to watch. If you think there aren't enough camels in Australia for a camel race, think again! The country has got about 150,000 wild camels. In the 19th century people used them for journeys when there wasn't enough water for

their horses. When railways and roads arrived, the camels weren't useful any more, but they survived very happily in Australia's central desert.

The other strange race at Alice Springs is the Henley-on-Todd Regatta. The name comes from a famous boat race at Henley-on-Thames in England. But there's one big difference. There's always water in the Thames – but the Todd River in Alice Springs is nearly always dry. They use boats without a bottom and teams of people run along the river bed, carrying their boats with them. If there's a lot of rain, the race doesn't take place because there's too much water in the river!

1 In Alice Springs
  a there are too many goats.
  b people aren't interested in sport.
  c there are two interesting races.

2 In May
  a the town is full of people.
  b two people always have a camel race.
  c there aren't many camels in Alice Springs.

3 In Australia 200 years ago,
  a camel racing was very popular.
  b there weren't enough horses.
  c people sometimes travelled on camels.

4 The Henley-on-Todd Regatta is
  a a funny boat race.
  b an unusual type of boat.
  c a race in England.

5 The Todd River
  a has often got more water than the Thames.
  b hasn't usually got any water.
  c has often got too much water.

4 Extension *Time to talk*

a **Emma is having a conversation with a friend. Read what she says.**

EMMA:
- How about going out somewhere on Saturday?
- Where shall we go? Have you got any suggestions?
- Oh, well ... no, I don't really want to do that. I'd rather go shopping.
- Great. So where shall we meet?
- All right then. What time?
- Fine. See you then.

🔊 **Now listen to the conversation.**

b **Read Emma's sentences again. Then imagine she's talking to you. Think about the answers <u>you</u> want to make.**

c 🔊 **Close your book, listen to the sentences and respond.**

'It's a hard life!': Vocabulary check

1 Some words have 'silent' letters, for example _write_. Look at the words in the box.
Can you find a word with two 'silent' letters?

In the word _____ we don't pronounce the letters _____ .

| pay | midnight | classmate | still | as well | get to | packed lunch | all the time | normal | extra |

2 Replace the <u>underlined</u> words so that the meaning stays the same. Use the words in the box in Exercise 1.

1 I watched a film on TV last night. I couldn't follow it because my mother talked <u>from the beginning of the film to the end</u>. _____

2 I had an egg for breakfast and I had some toast <u>too</u>. _____

3 I'm going to the gym tonight with a <u>friend in my class</u>. _____

4 A: I'm going to buy a ticket for the basketball match.

   B: Can you get <u>a second</u> ticket? I'd like to go.
   _an_ _____

5 We usually <u>arrive at</u> school at 8.45.
   _____

6 A: What time did you go to bed last night?

   B: Quite late. About <u>12 o'clock</u>. _____

7 Yesterday wasn't special. It was just <u>an ordinary</u> day. _a_ _____

8 I'm going for a walk in the mountains tomorrow. I'm going to take <u>some sandwiches and an apple to eat at lunchtime</u>. _a_ _____

9 Neil and Zoe are both over 30, but they <u>continue to</u> live with their parents. _____

10 A: I need a new bag for school.

   B: Don't worry. I'll <u>give you the money</u> for it.
   _____

3 Translate these sentences into your language.

1 A: Shall we look round the shops?
   B: Yes, that's fine with me.

   _____
   _____
   _____

2 A: How about going for a swim this afternoon?
   B: I'd rather go surfing. Why don't we take our surfboards as well?

   _____
   _____
   _____
   _____

3 Don't say 'I don't mind' all the time! Say yes or no.

   _____
   _____

4 It was a great party, but we made too much noise and the neighbours weren't very pleased.

   _____
   _____
   _____

5 I can't have lunch at the canteen. I haven't got enough money.

   _____
   _____

6 There are too many people on this bus. Let's walk into town.

   _____
   _____

Unit 4 Learning diary

Date _____

Now I know how to:

	Easy	Not bad	Difficult
• ask for suggestions.	☐	☐	☐

_____ shall we do? Where _____ go?

What time _____ ?

	Easy	Not bad	Difficult
• make suggestions.	☐	☐	☐

Let's _____ .

Shall we / Why don't we _____ ?

How about _____ ?

	Easy	Not bad	Difficult
• respond to suggestions.	☐	☐	☐

Shall we go swimming?   Yes, that's _____ .

How about playing volleyball? All _____ . / I don't _____ .

Why don't we watch TV?   I'd rather _____ .

	Easy	Not bad	Difficult
• talk about quantity.	☐	☐	☐

There's too _____ traffic.

There are too many _____ in the world.

There aren't enough _____ at my school.

	Easy	Not bad	Difficult
• write about a typical day.	☐	☐	☐

KEY WORDS

Places and buildings

mosque _____

_____

_____

_____

_____

_____

WORD WORK

get

get up = _____ (in my language)

get on the bus = _____   get dressed = _____

get off the train = _____   get to school = _____

get into the car = _____   get the bus = _____

get out of bed = _____   get a job = _____

get ready = _____

get home = _____

5 Goals

1 The future with the present continuous G➤6

Next Friday Jay's school football team is playing against Richmond School. Look at the notice. Then complete what Jay says about the arrangements. Use the present continuous (affirmative or negative).

> ### Under-18 football match at Richmond School
> ### Friday 12 November
>
> Teacher: ~~Mr Brown~~ Mr Jackson
>
> | | |
> |---|---|
> | 11.30 | Meet at school gate |
> | 11.40–12.15 | Bus to Richmond |
> | 12.30–1.30 | Lunch: Richmond School canteen |
> | 2.00–3.45 | Match |
> | 4.15 | Bus back to school |
> | 5.00 | Arrive at school |

The match [1] *is taking place* (take place) on Friday afternoon. The players [2] _____ (meet) Mr Jackson at 11.30 at the school gate and the bus [3] _____ (leave) at 11.40. Mr Brown [4] _____ (go) with us. I [5] _____ (take) any food because we [6] _____ (have) lunch in the school canteen at Richmond. The match [7] _____ (start) at two o'clock. After the match, the bus [8] _____ (bring) us back to school. We [9] _____ (arrive) at school at about five.

2 The future with *going to* G➤7

Write sentences with *going to*. Use a verb from box A and a noun from box B.

A	buy	catch
	play	clean
	visit	~~take~~

B	the 7.30 train	~~some photos~~
	his wife	some tickets
	basketball	her teeth

1 I've got my camera. _I'm going to take some photos_ .

2 Gina's at the sports centre. _____

_____ .

3 We're standing in the queue because _____

_____ .

4 Julie's in the bathroom. _____

_____ .

5 Mr Fletcher is at the hospital. _____

_____ .

6 Hana and Adel are waiting on the platform. _____

_____ .

3 *going to* and the present continuous G➤ 6.7

Match the sentences.

1 I've got a test on Thursday.
2 Mum's at the airport.
3 This top doesn't look very nice.
4 Isabel's got a seat on the train.
5 We must hurry.
6 It isn't cold today.
7 Let's go out next weekend.
8 Ann can't come to the gym tomorrow.

a I'm not going to wear it.
b The taxi's coming in five minutes.
c Are you doing anything on Saturday?
d She's going to the dentist.
e ~~I'm going to study in the library.~~
f She isn't coming by plane.
g My grandparents are arriving from Canada.
h I'm not going to take a coat.

1 _e_ 2 ____ 3 ____ 4 ____ 5 ____ 6 ____ 7 ____ 8 ____

4 Reading *Cheerleading*

Antonia is an American student and she's writing to her Spanish pen friend. Read her email.
Then read the sentences and write *T* (true), *F* (false) or *?* (the answer isn't in the text).

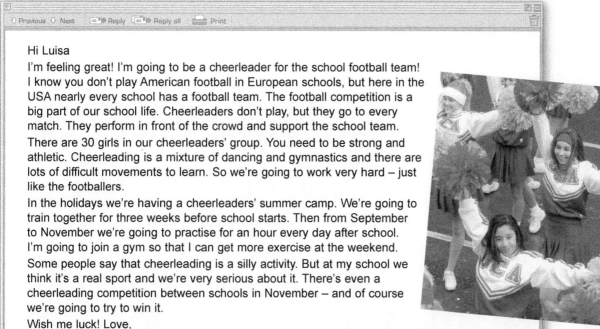

Hi Luisa

I'm feeling great! I'm going to be a cheerleader for the school football team!
I know you don't play American football in European schools, but here in the
USA nearly every school has a football team. The football competition is a
big part of our school life. Cheerleaders don't play, but they go to every
match. They perform in front of the crowd and support the school team.

There are 30 girls in our cheerleaders' group. You need to be strong and
athletic. Cheerleading is a mixture of dancing and gymnastics and there are
lots of difficult movements to learn. So we're going to work very hard – just
like the footballers.

In the holidays we're having a cheerleaders' summer camp. We're going to
train together for three weeks before school starts. Then from September
to November we're going to practise for an hour every day after school.
I'm going to join a gym so that I can get more exercise at the weekend.

Some people say that cheerleading is a silly activity. But at my school we
think it's a real sport and we're very serious about it. There's even a
cheerleading competition between schools in November – and of course
we're going to try to win it.

Wish me luck! Love,

Antonia

1 American football is a popular sport in schools all over the world. ____
2 Antonia is going to sit in the crowd at every football match. ____
3 Her school usually wins the football competition. ____
4 She's going away with other cheerleaders in the summer holidays. ____
5 The cheerleaders are going to practise five days a week in the autumn. ____
6 Antonia is a member of a gym. ____
7 She's going to be in a cheerleading competition. ____
8 Antonia's group will win the competition. ____

5 Extension *Your next holiday*

Imagine you're going on holiday to an interesting place next week. Write sentences in your notebook.

• Where are you going?
• How are you getting there?
• What are you going to take with you?
• What are you going to do at your destination?

I'm travelling to Egypt next week.
I'm going to spend five days in Cairo.

1 Key vocabulary *Sports clothes*

Complete the words for sports clothes.

1 Men don't wear trousers when they play tennis. They wear s_____ .

2 You often wear b_____ on your feet when you ride a horse.

3 Athletes often wear a t_____ when they're training. It's warm and comfortable.

4 At the swimming pool, boys wear swimming t_____ but girls wear a s_____ .

5 People often wear a w_____ when they're surfing. It's very useful when the water is cold.

6 You can see better in the water if you wear g_____ , and they protect your eyes.

7 Footballers wear long s_____ . They've got the team colours on them.

2 *will* for offers Ⓖ 5c

a What are these people saying? Match the sentences with the pictures.

a We're hungry.

b I can't find Land's End on this map.

c Look! It's Joanne's ring. She'll be worried about it.

d ~~I haven't got much music for the party.~~

e Look at this mess!

f I haven't got enough money.

1 *d*____ 2 ____ 3 ____ 4 ____ 5 ____ 6 ____

b Now make offers to help the people in the pictures in 2a. Use *I'll* + words from box A and box B.

A	make	phone	wash		B	you	~~some CDs~~	the floor	her
	show	~~bring~~	pay for			your ticket	some sandwiches		

1 *I'll bring some CDs.*_____

2 _____

3 _____

4 _____

5 _____

6 _____

3 *will* for decisions ⓖ➤ 5c

Look at these situations and make a decision (*I'll ...*). Use your own ideas.

1 It's a nice day and you want to get some exercise. *I think I'll go for a walk* .

2 You're thirsty. *I think* .

3 You've got a new poster for your room. *I'll* .

4 You want to contact an old friend. .

5 You aren't feeling well this morning. *I don't think* .

4 Listening *Making decisions*

🔊 Listen to the conversations with five people. What do they decide to do? Tick (✓) the right answer: A, B or C.

①

A ☐ B ☐ C ☐

②

A ☐ B ☐ C ☐

③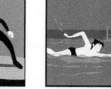

A ☐ B ☐ C ☐

④

A ☐ B ☐ C ☐

⑤

A ☐ B ☐ C ☐

5 Key expressions *Shopping*

Richard is talking to a shop assistant in a clothes shop. Complete the conversation.

ASSISTANT: Can I help you?

RICHARD: Oh, yes, please. I like this sweater, but I'm not sure about the colour. Have you got ¹ *a blue one* ?

ASSISTANT: No, sorry, we haven't got any blue ones – only black or brown.

RICHARD: Oh well, the black one's OK. ² _____ ?

ASSISTANT: It's £36.

RICHARD: I'm not sure if it's ³ _____ for me. It looks too small.

ASSISTANT: What ⁴ _____ ?

RICHARD: Medium.

ASSISTANT: Yes, that one's too small. This one's medium.

RICHARD: Oh, good. ⁵ _____ ?

ASSISTANT: Yes, sure. The fitting room's over there in the corner.

6 Extension *Clothes and equipment*

What's your favourite sport? In your notebook, write a list of the clothes and equipment you need for your sport. Use a dictionary if necessary.

Tennis: shorts, tennis shoes, racket ...

'High hopes!': Vocabulary check

1 Look at the words in the box. Can you find eight adjectives?

Adjectives: _____ _____

_____ _____ _____

_____ _____ _____

jump	lazy	achievement	high jumper
ambitious	especially	forgetful	afraid
irritating	medal	honest	performance
successful	admire	well-paid	enter

2 Use the adjectives in the box in Exercise 1 to describe these people.

1 My little sister always tries to annoy me. She drives me mad.

   irritating

2 Sally often dreams about her future. She doesn't want an ordinary career. She wants to be the first woman on Mars.

   _____

3 It's midnight. Jack can hear a noise outside his tent, but he doesn't want to go out because he hates the dark.

   _____

4 Rory doesn't do any sport. He doesn't help in the house. He just sits in front of the TV all evening.

   _____

5 My brother has got a boring job, but he earns a lot of money.

   _____

6 There's a note in Polly's diary: 'Dentist 2 pm'. It's two o'clock now and Polly's sitting in a café with a friend.

   _____

7 At school my uncle passed all his exams. After school he played rugby for England. Then he became a famous film director.

   _____

8 My gran said to me: 'Always tell the truth. It's the best thing to do.'

   _____

3 Translate these sentences into your language.

1 I play basketball for my college team. We're playing against Stanford next Saturday.

   _____

2 I really like that swimsuit. I think I'll try it on. Where's the fitting room?

   _____

3 Tom's raising money for a charity. He's going to ride his motorbike across the Sahara Desert.

   _____

4 What's in this bag? Is it your new wetsuit? Can I have a look?

   _____

5 I really admire Catherine. She's very ambitious and she isn't afraid of anything.

   _____

6 A: Have you got everything?
   B: Yes. I've got my swimming trunks, my goggles and some money for the pool.

   _____

Unit 5 Learning diary

Date _____

Now I know how to:

	Easy	Not bad	Difficult

- talk about arrangements for the future. ☐ ☐ ☐

  What are you doing on Sunday?

  I _____ .

- talk about plans. ☐ ☐ ☐

  What's the next thing you're going to buy?

  I _____ .

  There's a horror film on TV tonight, but I _____ it.

- use *will* for decisions. ☐ ☐ ☐

  I think I'll _____ tonight.

  I don't think I _____ tomorrow.

- make an offer. ☐ ☐ ☐

  Don't worry. I'll _____ for you.

- ask about things in a shop. ☐ ☐ ☐

  How _____ that T-shirt? Can _____ it on?

  I don't like yellow. Have _____ one?

- interview a friend and then write about him/her. ☐ ☐ ☐

KEY WORDS

Sports clothes

goggles _____ _____

_____ _____

_____ _____

_____

WORD WORK

Adjective or verb + preposition

good	+ *at*
worry	+ _____
interested	+ _____
bad	+ _____
listen	+ _____
afraid	+ _____

1 Key vocabulary *At the table*

Look at the pictures and complete the crossword.

2 will/won't be able to Ⓖ→ 5e

Match the sentences.

1 Lee's got a bad cold.
2 Gran gave us her recipe for apple cake.
3 They aren't showing the match on TV.
4 This bag is very heavy!
5 Greg isn't doing anything tomorrow.
6 Lisa dropped her phone from the upstairs window.
7 My cousins are coming to the barbecue.
8 Jane got good results in all her exams.

a We'll be able to make one this weekend.
b She won't be able to mend it.
c She'll be able to go to university.
d He won't be able to go swimming tomorrow.
e You'll be able to meet them.
f He'll be able to take us to the beach in his car.
g You won't be able to carry it very far.
h We won't be able to watch it.

1 __*d*__ 2 _____ 3 _____ 4 _____ 5 _____ 6 _____ 7 _____ 8 _____

3 First conditional G→8

Alex is talking about his girlfriend to his friend Luke. Complete the conversation. Circle the right answer: a, b or c.

ALEX: I'm really fed up, Luke. I think Suzie fancies Brian Carey.

LUKE: But she's your girlfriend.

ALEX: Look. I found this photo of him in her bag.

LUKE: Did you take that from Suzie's bag? ¹_____ really angry if she finds out.

ALEX: She won't find out if ²_____ tell her. Anyway, it doesn't matter. She ³_____ to take lots more photos of Brian if she ⁴_____ to go out with him. And she won't ⁵_____ to hide them in her bag.

LUKE: Hang on. She's coming into the classroom. She looks worried.

SUZIE: Alex! I had a photo in my bag and now I can't find it. It's a photo of Brian Carey for the school magazine. They need it this afternoon. If ⁶_____ find it, they ⁷_____ able to finish the page, and if they ⁸_____ finish the page, ⁹_____ really annoyed with me.

LUKE: Alex, I think you've got a few things to explain.

	a	b	c
1	a She's	(b) She'll be	c She was
2	a you don't	b you won't	c you'll
3	a can	b 'll	c 'll be able
4	a 'll decide	b decides	c decide
5	a need	b needs	c to need
6	a I	b I'll	c I don't
7	a 're	b aren't	c won't be
8	a aren't	b can't	c can
9	a they'll be	b they be	c they're

4 Key expressions *Polite requests*

Complete the requests.

1 Can _I have some crisps, please_ ?

2 Could _____ ?

3 I _____ .

4 Could _____ ?

5 I _____ .

6 Could _____ ?

5 Listening *Ordering a meal*

🔊 Becky, Adam and their father are ordering lunch at a café. What are they going to have? Listen and write three letters (a–k) in the boxes for each person.

1 Becky [d] [ ] [ ]

2 Adam [ ] [ ] [ ]

3 Dad [ ] [ ] [ ]

a vegetable soup	g	steak
b chicken soup	h	chips
c pâté	i	potatoes
d ~~lasagne~~	j	salad
e fish	k	ice cream
f chicken		

6 Extension *Odd one out*

Which word is the odd one out?

1 dessert (meal) main course starter
2 knife spoon serviette fork
3 plate cup glass bottle
4 melon carrot orange apple
5 salt ketchup pepper soup
6 chips mushrooms vegetarians peas
7 steak chicken ham tart
8 rice cheese cream butter

1 will / won't for promises 5c

Complete each reply with a promise.
Use *will* or *won't* with the words in the box.

> send you an email   come in a minute
> visit you again   be late   ~~forget~~   hurt

① REMEMBER – CLOSE THE WINDOWS BEFORE YOU GO OUT.

② YOU MUST BE HOME BEFORE MIDNIGHT.

③ THANKS A LOT FOR COMING.

④ WILL YOU WRITE TO ME?

⑤ I'M A BIT NERVOUS ABOUT THIS.

⑥ I'D LIKE SOME HELP IN THE KITCHEN, PLEASE.

1 OK, Mum. I *won't forget* .

2 Yes, I know. I _____ .

3 We _____ on Saturday.

4 Yes, I _____ every day.

5 Don't worry. I promise it _____ .

6 OK. I _____ .

2 might / might not 10

Complete the sentences. Use *might* or *might not* with the verbs in the box.

> agree   have   ~~be~~   go   snow   belong

1 There were television cameras at our school today.
   We *might be* _____ on TV!

2 It's very cold. I think it _____ soon.

3 I'm not sure what I'll have for lunch. I had a big
   breakfast, so I _____ anything.

4 A: Will we see Danny on Friday?
   B: I don't know. _____ to the disco.
      He didn't enjoy it last week.

5 A: Whose are these sunglasses?
   B: I'm not sure. They _____ to Paula.

6 I think this band is great, but you _____
   _____ . Lots of people don't like them.

3 'll / won't and might / might not
 5b, 10

Write the sentences in a different way. Use *'ll, won't, might* or *might not*.

1 Maybe Maria won't pass her science exam.
   Maria *might fail* _____ her science exam.

2 I don't think Kate's friends will be at the party.
   Kate's friends probably _____ to the
   party.

3 I'm not sure I can pay for both these books.
   I _____ enough money for both
   these books.

4 I'm always nervous when I'm in a car, so I probably
   won't be a good driver.
   I'm always nervous when I'm in a car, so I don't
   think I _____ at driving.

5 Perhaps Gerard's parents will give him a surfboard.
   Gerard _____ a surfboard from
   his parents.

4 Reading *Ideas about the future*

Read the article from a school magazine. Then complete the sentences with the right name: *Gemma* or *Nick*.

Looking into the future ...

Gemma Lyons, 15

Job: I'm not interested in going to university when I leave school, but I'm not going to work in an office or a shop. I'll get a job outdoors if I can. I like working with plants, so I'll probably look for a job as a gardener. The money might not be great, but I'll enjoy the work. And one day I might be able to grow my own plants and sell them. I'd like to have my own business.

Home: I really want to be independent, but I won't be able to leave home for a few years. One day I'll get a little flat on my own. I don't think I'll move away from this town. It's nice here and I'd like to stay near my family.

Nick Sanderson, 16

Job: I think I'll be able to do a science course at university and I'd like to get a job that helps the environment. But I don't think it'll be easy to find an interesting job. I'd love to study whales or dolphins, but that will be difficult. There's a lot of competition for jobs like that.

Home: I'll probably share a house with other students when I'm at university. After that, I'm not sure where I'll live. I might not be able to find work here. If someone offers me a good job in another country, perhaps I'll take it.

1 .... will probably study at university.

2 .... doesn't want to work inside.

3 .... is optimistic about finding a job.

4 .... is quite ambitious.

5 .... won't live at home after his/her final year at school.

6 .... wants to live alone.

7 .... might live abroad.

8 .... is more confident about the future than ....

5 Extension *Time to talk*

MENU

Starters

Mushroom soup

Melon with ham

Tomato salad

Main courses

Steak with chips and salad

Chicken with mushroom sauce

Cheese and onion tart

Desserts

Apple pie and cream

Ice cream (chocolate or coffee)

a Patrick is having a conversation with a friend in a café. Read what he says and what the waiter says.

PATRICK:

- I think I'll start with tomato salad. Are you going to have a starter?
- What about the main course?
- Yes, that'll be nice. And I might have some chocolate ice cream for dessert. What about you?
- The waiter's coming now. Are you ready?

WAITER:

- Would you like to order?

🔊 Now listen to the conversation.

b Read the sentences again. Then imagine Patrick and the waiter are talking to you. Look at the menu and think about the answers <u>you</u> want to make.

c 🔊 Close your book, listen to the sentences and respond.

'Artificial Intelligence': Vocabulary check

1 Look at the words in the box. Find three compound nouns.

Compound nouns: _____   _____

_____

| washing machine improve laboratory common own |
| oven grow up coffee maker develop computer chip |

2 Match sentences 1–10 with sentences a–j.

1 Scientists are developing a rocket plane.
2 Luís spent six months in London.
3 My aunt works in a laboratory.
4 My coffee maker's broken.
5 Look at my jeans – they're really dirty.
6 People all over the world use mobiles.
7 I can't cook this chicken.
8 Ellie's growing up fast.
9 My brother has got his own flat now.
10 Modern machines have got brains.

a I'll put them in the washing machine.
b She isn't a little girl any more.
c ~~One day people will fly from London to Sydney in two hours.~~
d He doesn't live with us any more.
e They're called computer chips.
f She makes robots for the European Space Project.
g His English has improved a lot.
h They're very common now.
i The oven doesn't work.
j What about a cup of tea?

1 _c_   2 ____   3 ____   4 ____   5 ____   6 ____   7 ____   8 ____   9 ____   10 ____

3 Translate these sentences into your language.

1 Could you pass me the salt and pepper, Dad?

2 A: What would you like for your main course?
B: I'll have fish and chips, please.

3 A: Remember! Phone me at eight o'clock.
B: I promise I won't forget.

4 A: If you go to live in Australia, I'll miss you.
B: Don't worry. I might not go.

5 If you don't finish your spaghetti, the dog will probably eat it.

6 If I don't catch the last bus, I won't be able to get home.

Unit 6 Learning diary

Date _____

Now I know how to:

	Easy	Not bad	Difficult
talk about possibilities and results.	☐	☐	☐

If I'm lucky, I'll _____ .

If _____ , *I won't be very happy.*

	Easy	Not bad	Difficult
make polite requests.	☐	☐	☐

I'm hungry. Can I _____ ?

Could I _____ ?

Could you _____ ?

	Easy	Not bad	Difficult
make promises.	☐	☐	☐

I'll phone you tonight. Don't worry. I _____ *forget.*

I _____ . *I promise.*

	Easy	Not bad	Difficult
talk about things that are probable or uncertain.	☐	☐	☐

I'll probably _____ .

I probably won't _____ .

I might _____ *but I'm not sure.*

I might not _____ .

	Easy	Not bad	Difficult
write about life in the future.	☐	☐	☐

KEY WORDS
At the table

plate _____ _____

_____ _____

_____ _____

_____ _____

WORD WORK
Compound nouns

washing machine _____

_____ _____

_____ _____

_____ _____

7 Achievements

1 Present perfect: affirmative 11a

a Complete the table.

Verb	Past simple	Past participle
invent	invented	[1] *invented*
arrive	arrived	[2]
drop	[3]	dropped
[4]	bought	bought
do	[5]	[6]
[7]	broke	[8]
take	[9]	[10]
[11]	forgot	[12]

b Look at the pictures. What have these people done? Write sentences with the words in the box and verbs from 1a.

> her keys   the window   a new machine
> your scarf   ~~some new shoes~~   the shopping

1 *I've bought some new shoes.*

2 *He*

3 *You*

4 *She*

5 *They*

6 *I*

2 Present perfect: negative 11a

Complete the sentences. Use the verbs in the negative form of the present perfect.

1 We can't sing that song. We __*haven't learnt*__ the words. (*learn*)

2 Ana's still upstairs. She _____ her letter to her sister. (*finish*)

3 Kate's got a new boyfriend, but I _____ _____ him. (*meet*)

4 Mrs Grant's annoyed because Charlie _____ _____ the washing up. (*do*)

5 The new band *Hot Metal* is popular in the clubs, but they _____ a record. (*make*)

6 A: My mobile's disappeared. Where is it?
   B: I don't know. I _____ it. (*take*)

7 Jay isn't here at the moment. He _____ _____ from the shops. (*come back*)

3 Reading *Park Rescue*

Read the text about Michael Chambers and the group he has organised. Then read the sentences and write *T* (true), *F* (false) or *?* (the answer isn't in the text).

A SHORT TIME AGO, the local park in Selwood looked terrible. The lake was polluted, seats were broken and the place was full of rubbish.

But now all that has changed, thanks to Michael Chambers, a 16-year-old student. Six months ago, Michael organised a group called Park Rescue, and this group has produced some amazing results.

Members have used their free time to clean the park. They've taken away tons of rubbish, and they've started to clean the lake. They've mended a lot of the seats and they've bought some new picnic tables. They've also planted some flowers and 60 young trees.

Michael has talked about the project on the radio and he's put articles in the local newspaper. In six months, about 120 people have joined Park Rescue. The group has organised concerts and they've collected money in the street. With these activities and with the help of some local business people, they've raised over £4,000.

'We haven't finished the work,' Michael says. 'We want to make a skateboarding area, and at the moment we need some advice about cleaning the lake. But birds have started to come back to Selwood Park, and it's becoming a place that people can enjoy. The old café is going to open soon and that will be great.'

If you can help, contact Michael on 01623 449280 or at parkrescue@biglink.co.uk.

1 Park Rescue started six months ago. ....
2 Michael got a job at Selwood Park. ....
3 There's a lot of rubbish in the park at the moment. ....
4 Michael's group hasn't finished cleaning the lake. ....
5 Michael has appeared on television. ....
6 There are over a hundred people in the Park Rescue group now. ....
7 They want to organise more concerts. ....
8 They need to get £4,000 for their work in the park. ....
9 There have always been lots of birds in the park. ....

4 Present perfect: questions (G)→ 11a

Read the replies in this conversation about Selwood Park. Then write the questions using the present perfect.

A: ¹ *Have* Michael and his group

  cleaned the lake ?

B: No, but they've started to clean it.

A: ²What _____ ?

B: Some picnic tables.

A: ³How _____

  _____ ?

B: About 120.

A: ⁴ _____

  _____ ?

B: Over £4,000.

A: ⁵ _____

  a skateboarding area?

B: No, they haven't.

A: ⁶ _____ ?

B: No, it hasn't, but it's going to open soon.

A: ⁷ _____ the park _____ ?

B: Oh, yes! It's improved a lot.

5 Extension

What's happened in your life?

Think about things that have happened in the past six months. In your notebook, write sentences in the present perfect.

Things I'm proud of:
I've learnt to dive.

Things I'm not proud of:
I've argued a lot with my dad.

Things I'm happy about:
I've made some new friends at school.

Things I'm unhappy about:
My favourite TV programme has finished.

1 Key vocabulary

Using a machine 21

Read the sentences and <u>underline</u> the right words.

1 Don't forget to turn the lights (*on* / <u>*off*</u>) before you go to bed.
2 It's an electric keyboard. It won't work if you don't plug it (*in* / *on*).
3 The meal will be ready in ten minutes if we (*put* / *take*) it in the microwave.
4 You'll see a light on the front of the computer when you turn it (*on* / *off*).
5 Your jeans are in the washing machine. You can't take them (*off* / *out*) until the machine has stopped.
6 If there's a big storm, it's a good idea to (*unplug* / *plug in*) your computer.

2 Present perfect and past simple

 11b, 12

Complete the sentences. Use one verb in the present perfect and the other in the past simple.

1 I ___*noticed*___ (*notice*) that magazine in the newsagent's yesterday, but I ___*haven't read*___ (*not read*) it.

2 Oh, wow! You _____ (*buy*) a new jacket. When _____ you _____ (*get*) it?

3 Cathy _____ (*take*) her umbrella with her when she left home, but now she thinks she _____ (*lose*) it.

4 Alex! You _____ (*not take*) your tablets! I _____ (*put*) them by your bed this morning.

5 My sister _____ (*drop*) my sunglasses and broke them. I'm not angry with her because she _____ (*promise*) to buy me a new pair.

6 Our neighbours are worried because their cat _____ (*not come*) home. It _____ (*disappear*) last Friday.

3 Present perfect and past simple 11b, 12

Complete the conversations. Use the present perfect or the past simple form of the verbs in each box.

1

| buy   make |

A: Look! Dad ___*'s made*___ a cake!

B: I don't believe it. I think he ___*bought*___ it on his way home.

2

| explain   forget   finish |

A: _____ you _____ your maths homework?

B: No, I haven't. I can't do it. The teacher _____ it to me yesterday, but now I _____ _____ what he said.

3

| hit   break   happen |

A: Irena _____ her arm.

B: Oh, no. How _____ that _____ ?

A: She _____ a tree when she was riding her bike.

4

| think   watch   hate |

A: _____ Steve _____ this video?

B: Yes, he has.

A: What _____ he _____ of it?

B: He _____ it.

4 Listening

A news report

🔊 Listen to the local news report on a Bristol radio station. Tick (✓) the right answer: a, b or c.

1 The police have
  a destroyed a factory. ☐
  b discovered how the fire started. ☐
  c closed the street. ☐

2 Greg Jones has
  a saved his sister. ☐
  b had a dangerous accident. ☐
  c helped his family. ☐

3 Mr Spencer has
  a bought some paintings. ☐
  b lost a lot of money. ☐
  c done a lot of painting. ☐

4 *Wild Roses*
  a have visited a hospital. ☐
  b are in hospital. ☐
  c have used a machine at the hospital. ☐

5 Graham McShann hasn't
  a moved to Middlesbrough. ☐
  b scored many goals. ☐
  c decided to leave Bristol City. ☐

6 Extension *Poem*

🔊 Find the past participles by adding *a, e, i, o* or *u* and complete the poem. Then listen to the poem and read it aloud.

tkn	blt	trvlld	lrnt	~~sld~~	stdd	lndd

I've ¹ _sailed_ along the Amazon,

I've ² _____ by balloon,

I've ³ _____ flights to outer space,

I've ⁴ _____ on the moon,

But still somehow I find

I can't leave you behind.

I've ⁵ _____ eleven languages,

I've ⁶ _____ a bridge or two,

I've ⁷ _____ Chinese writing and

The history of Peru,

But still somehow I find

You're always on my mind.

5 Key expressions *I think so / I don't think so*

Write the replies. Choose the right sentences (a–f) and use them with *I think so* or *I don't think so*.

1 A: Is that Ben over there?
  B: *I don't think so. He doesn't live near here.*

2 A: Does this camera work?
  B: _____

3 A: Is Sarah coming home from hospital soon?
  B: _____

4 A: Will your brothers be at the match tomorrow?
  B: _____

5 A: Is Tony still going out with Caroline?
  B: _____

6 A: Has Emma finished the washing up?
  B: _____

a She's getting better now.

b But you need to turn it on.

c She's still in the kitchen.

d ~~He doesn't live near here.~~

e They aren't great sports fans.

f I saw them together a few days ago.

'Take Action!': Vocabulary check

1 Match the words in the box with the correct stress.

endangered	plant	injured	campaign
channels	volunteers	determined	protect

1 ●●● _volunteers_

2 ●

3 ●●●

4 ●●

5 ●●

2 Complete the answers. Use the words in the box in Exercise 1.

1 There aren't many trees on the hill. When it rains, all the soil comes down the hill into the village. What should the people do?

They should _plant more trees._

2 You want to start a new music club. You need people to help you. What are you looking for?

I'm looking for

3 A lion is attacking a cheetah. The cheetah is standing in front of its three babies. What's it trying to do?

It's trying to

4 The gorra-gorra bird is disappearing. There are now only twenty-five in the world. Why are wildlife experts worried?

Because the gorra-gorra bird

5 The footballer Jimmy Blix fell down the stairs yesterday. Why can't he play next Saturday?

Because he

6 Eva Smith has tried five times to sail round the world. She hasn't been successful, but she's going to try again next week. How do you describe a girl like Eva?

She's a very

7 The students and the teachers are having a meeting. The road next to their school is dangerous and they want a bridge across the road. What are they going to do?

They're going to start

8 What are these? BBC 1, CNN, Sky News, MTV.

They're TV

3 Translate these sentences into your language.

1 A: Have you seen the advert for Ford cars on TV?

B: Yes, I have. It's very funny.

2 Kirsty doesn't take care of her things. She's broken her new stereo.

3 You've turned the television on and I'm trying to read! Don't be selfish!

4 A: Has Kelly come home?

B: No, I don't think so. I haven't seen her.

5 A: Did you turn the oven off when you left the house?

B: Yes, I think so.

6 Have you unplugged your computer? They say in the instructions: 'Always unplug your computer when there's a storm.'

Unit 7 Learning diary

Now I know how to:

	Easy	Not bad	Difficult

- describe achievements. ☐ ☐ ☐

  _____ you finished your homework?

  My friend _____ started a campaign.

  I'm very proud because I've _____ .

- talk about what people have done and when/where they did it. ☐ ☐ ☐

  Pete has _____ his mobile. He left it on the bus yesterday.

  Charlie _____ the washing up. He _____ it after dinner.

- explain the purpose of something. ☐ ☐ ☐

  It's a campaign to _____ .

  I'm saving my money _____ .

- write a letter about a campaign. ☐ ☐ ☐

KEY WORDS

Using a machine

(turn on)
Turn the television on. = _____ (in my language)

(turn off)
Turn it off! = _____

(take out)
Take the plug out. = _____

(put in)
Put the disc in. = _____

(unplug)
Unplug your computer. = _____

(plug in)
Plug it in. = _____

8 Experiences

1 Key vocabulary *Outdoor activities*

Complete the sentences with outdoor activities.

1 You use a surfboard when you go s_____ .

2 When you do a b_____ - j_____ , you fall with your head down.

3 You usually travel down a river when you go c_____ .

4 S_____ is like surfing on the snow.

5 If you go s_____ - d_____ , you can see some fascinating things under the sea.

6 Kids often practise s_____ in the park or in the street.

7 If you're good at c_____ , you can get to the top of a mountain.

8 S_____ is a great sport for people who like boats.

2 Present perfect + *ever* and *never*

G→ 11c

Complete the sentences. Use the verbs in the present perfect. Use *ever* in the questions and *never* in the answers.

1 A: _____*Have*_____ you _____*ever stayed*_____ at the Blue Lake campsite? (*stay*)

   B: No, _*I haven't*_ . _*I've never been*_ there. (*be*)

2 A: _____ you _____ a mountain bike? (*ride*)

   B: No, _____ . I _____ _____ to ride a bike. (*learn*)

3 A: _____ Fiona _____ a pizza? (*make*)

   B: No, _____ . She _____ _____ a meal. (*cook*)

3 Present perfect + *just*

G→ 11d

Complete the sentences about what has just happened. Use *just* with the present perfect form of the verbs in box A and the words in box B.

A	learn	see
	swim	be
	~~mend~~	fall

B	to China	~~his motorbike~~
	to walk	asleep
	400 metres	a ghost

1 Danny _*has just mended his motorbike*_ .

2 I _____ .

3 Frank _____ .

4 We _____ .

5 Sam _____ .

6 They _____ .

4 Listening *What have they done?*

🔊 Listen to the conversation between Rosa and Gary. What have the five people done? Write the letters a–e.

1	Rosa	c	a has bought some sports clothes
2	Megan	☐	b has done a bungee-jump
3	Jay	☐	~~c has been canoeing~~
4	Tom	☐	d has painted some pictures
5	Gary	☐	e has played basketball

5 Make a conversation

Read the information and write the conversation.

Sue and Paul are talking about holidays.

SUPER SKIING HOLIDAYS

1 Sue asks Paul if he's ever been skiing.
2 Paul says yes – he tried it once when he was in France.
3 Sue asks Paul when he went to France.
4 Paul says that he went there a year ago with his uncle. He asks Sue if she's ever been to France.
5 Sue replies that she hasn't, but she would like to go there one day. She asks Paul if he travels a lot with his family.
6 Paul replies that he doesn't, but he's been abroad twice.
7 Sue says that he's lucky. She tells him that she's never travelled outside England and she's never been on a plane.

SUE: ¹ *Have you ever been skiing?*

PAUL: ²

SUE: ³

PAUL: ⁴

SUE: ⁵

PAUL: ⁶

SUE: ⁷

6 Extension

What are their jobs?

Read the sentences. Put the letters in the right order and find the people's jobs.

renarit	crotod	scrates
sub revird	phos stasnista	

1 Stefan hasn't got a car, but he's just driven to the airport.

----

2 Daniel goes to a clothes shop every day, but he's never bought anything there.

----

3 Jill has just come home from the hospital, but she hasn't been ill.

----

4 Ken has just been to the Olympic Games with the swimming team, but he didn't swim.

----

5 Liz has never been married, but she's had 15 different names.

----

1 Key expressions *Time expressions with* for *and* since   11e

Complete the sentences with the time expressions in the box.

ages   several months
the day before yesterday
last weekend   a few weeks
the Saturday before last
a couple of days

It's Wednesday 20th October.

1 Sarah started her job on Monday.

   She's had the job since _____ .

2 Hassan left on Monday. He's been away for _____ .

3 Greg's last football match was on 9th October. He hasn't played since _____ .

4 My grandparents came to this town a long time ago. They've lived here for _____ .

5 Alicia met Harry at the beginning of October. She's known him for _____ .

6 They arrived in Toronto in June or July. They've been in Canada for _____ .

7 Emma began to feel ill on Sunday. She's been ill since _____ .

2 Reading *A young musician*

a Read the article and complete it with *for* or *since*.

Success for young musician

¹ __For__ a long time Sharon Sadler has had a dream about playing in a big orchestra. Now her dream is coming true. At the age of 15, Sharon has just become the youngest member of the Brighton Orchestra.

Sharon has played the violin ² _____ she was five years old and she has studied with her teacher, Janet Chandler, ³ _____ eight years. 'Sharon was a brilliant player even when she was a little girl,' Mrs Chandler said. 'But she's also worked incredibly hard. She's practised regularly ⁴ _____ several hours

every day and she's done her normal school work as well. Everyone's very proud of her.'

Sharon has been a star in the orchestra at the Kingsgate Music School ⁵ _____ she joined it three years ago. She has performed in lots of local concerts and she won the Young Musicians competition last May. ⁶ _____ the competition, she has appeared several times on national television.

Sharon is beginning her work with the Brighton Orchestra next month. She has got special permission to be

out of school when the orchestra is practising. 'It's so exciting,' Sharon said. 'This has been my ambition ⁷ _____ years. It's hard to believe it's really happening.'

She's a young person with a great future. We wish her lots of success in her career.

b Read the text again. Then read the sentences and circle the right answer: a, b or c.

1 Sharon has just
   a had her fourteenth birthday.
   b started playing the violin.
   c joined a big orchestra.

2 She's had violin lessons with Mrs Chandler since she was
   a five.
   b seven.
   c eight.

3 She hasn't
   a done much school work.
   b finished school.
   c been very hard-working.

4 She's been a member of her school orchestra
   a for three years.
   b for 18 months.
   c for eight years.

5 Sharon's first performance on TV was
   a in May.
   b before May.
   c after May.

6 At the moment she's
   a planning to leave school.
   b practising with the Brighton Orchestra.
   c feeling excited about the future.

3 Questions in the present perfect (G) 11a

Put the words in the right order and make questions. Then match them with the answers (a–f).

1 good / have / any / recently / seen / films / you ?

Have you seen any good films recently? ...c..

2 your / tried / friends / have / skateboarding / ever ?

....

3 coffee / new / Dad / has / a / maker / bought ?

....

4 known / Sandra / long / you / how / have ?

....

5 long / London / for / time / lived / Helen / a / has / in ?

....

6 camping / times / you / many / been / have / how ?

....

a	Since September.
b	Four or five times.
~~c~~	~~No, I haven't.~~
d	Yes, she's been here for ten years.
e	No, they haven't.
f	Yes, he has.

4 for, since and just (G) 11d, 11e

Write the sentences in a different way. Use *for*, *since* or *just*.

1 Jay met Ana last September.

Jay has *known Ana since last September* . (*know*)

2 Mr and Mrs Grant's home has been in London for 30 years.

Mr and Mrs Grant have ....

.... (*live*)

3 Ana went into her room two hours ago.

Ana has .... (*be*)

4 Martin finished his lunch a couple of minutes ago.

Martin has .... (*finish*)

5 I got this watch in January.

I've .... (*have*)

6 Lizzie's seventeen. Her interest in Africa started when she was eight years old.

Lizzie's seventeen. She's .... interested ....

.... (*be*)

7 Charlie started his exam five minutes ago.

Charlie has .... (*start*)

5 Extension *Time to talk*

a Sara is having a conversation with a new friend. Read what she says.

SARA:

- Have you lived here all your life?
- Have you ever travelled abroad?
- How long have you been at your school?
- Have you enjoyed studying English?
- What's your favourite sport?
- Have you ever played in a school competition?

Now listen to the conversation.

b Read Sara's questions again. Then imagine she's talking to you. Think about the answers you want to make.

c Close your book, listen to the questions and respond.

'U2 – The World's Biggest Band': Vocabulary check

1 Look at the words in the box. Can you find one adjective?

biography	awards
huge	field	including
fight	album	AIDS
perform	success	

Adjective: ....

2 Complete the sentences. Use words in the box in Exercise 1.

1 Look at those two lions. They're both really angry. I think they're going to ....

2 Millions of people all over the world have got .... , but they haven't all got the best medicine for it.

3 I like singing, but I'm shy. I don't want to .... in front of a lot of people.

4 Lizzie's party was a great .... The food and the music were fantastic. Everyone enjoyed it.

5 I've just read Elvis Presley's .... He had an incredible life.

6 Have you heard Joss Stone's new .... ? There are some fabulous new songs.

7 I'm not going to walk across that .... I'm afraid of cows.

8 My friend Kirsty's a brilliant piano player. She's won two .... – The Beethoven Piano Prize and Young Musician of the Year.

9 I was in a group with five other people. So there were six people in the group, ... me.

10 The blue whale's tongue is as big as an African elephant! It's ....

3 Translate these sentences into your language.

1 A: Have you ever tried scuba-diving?
B: No, I haven't. I've always been afraid of sharks.

....

....

....

....

2 My grandfather has never been abroad. But he's just decided to go to Paris for a week.

....

....

....

3 A: What's the matter?
B: I've just seen an enormous spider under the bed.

....

....

....

4 A: My mobile doesn't work.
B: How long have you had it?

....

....

....

5 A: How long have you known Monica?
B: I've known her for a long time. We've been friends since we started school.

....

....

....

....

6 AIDS is a huge problem for the world.

....

....

Unit 8 Learning diary

Date _____

Now I know how to:

	Easy	Not bad	Difficult
talk about experiences.	☐	☐	☐

I've never _____ .

Have you ever _____ ?

	Easy	Not bad	Difficult
describe things that happened a short time ago.	☐	☐	☐

The film has just _____ .

I've just _____ .

	Easy	Not bad	Difficult
ask how long present situations have continued.	☐	☐	☐

How long have you _____ ?

	Easy	Not bad	Difficult
say how long present situations have continued.	☐	☐	☐

I've _____ *for* _____ .

I've _____ *since* _____ .

	Easy	Not bad	Difficult
write a biography.	☐	☐	☐

KEY WORDS

Outdoor activities

scuba-diving _____

_____

_____

_____

_____

_____

_____

WORD WORK

Prepositions of time: *in, at, on*

at _____ five o'clock

_____ July

_____ Thursday

_____ summer

_____ 4th August

_____ Easter

_____ 1998

_____ midnight

Getting it right

1 *have to* and *don't have to* 14, 15

Katie and Nick are talking about their weekend jobs.
Complete the texts with *have/has to* and *don't/doesn't have to*.

KATIE

My dad's a baker and I ¹ _have to_ help him in the shop at the weekend. I ² _____ wear any special clothes, but I ³ _____ look tidy. A shop assistant ⁴ _____ be polite to customers and that isn't always easy. But the worst thing is that I ⁵ _____ get up very early and I hate that! Mum says I'm lazy. She works as a volunteer in the Oxfam charity shop. She ⁶ _____ work there, but she enjoys doing it.

NICK

I've got a weekend job at the Roseville Restaurant. You ⁷ _____ be energetic to be a waiter there. We serve about 150 meals at lunchtime and we ⁸ _____ be on our feet for about three hours. My friend Eddie works in the kitchen. He ⁹ _____ cook, but he has to cut up the vegetables and make the salads. It's nice when the customers have left. We all sit down together for a late lunch, and we ¹⁰ _____ pay for the meal.

2 *don't have to* and *mustn't* 15

These sentences are wrong! Correct them using *don't/doesn't have to* or *mustn't*.

1 You ~~have to~~ steal things from other people. _____ mustn't _____

2 People have to touch the paintings in an art gallery. _____

3 A teacher has to wear a uniform. _____

4 You have to put cheese in an omelette. _____

5 If you've got a computer, you have to write with a pen. _____

6 I have to be late for my job interview tomorrow. _____

7 You have to talk to other students when you're doing an exam. _____

8 An actor has to be good at maths and science. _____

3 *have to, don't have to* and *mustn't* Ⓖ▸ 14. 15

Match the sentences with the signs and complete the sentences. Use *have to, don't have to* or *mustn't*.

1 You __mustn't__ ride a bike on this road.   _b_

2 When people work here, they .... wear goggles to protect their eyes.   ....

3 We can go faster now. We .... drive at forty kilometres an hour.   ....

4 We .... be careful. We .... drive too fast because there might be camels on the road.   ....

4 Reading *Labels and adverts*

a Where can you find these texts? Write the letters A–D.

1 on a bottle in a chemist's ☐
2 in a national newspaper ☐
3 on an Internet website ☐
4 in a local newspaper ☐

Ⓐ **UK Short Story Writing Competition**

Prize: £2,500

Open to young people aged 12–18
Max. length for stories: 3,000 words
Closing date: 30 October

For further information and entry form, write to:
UK Young Writers Competition
PO Box 40
Cambridge CB1 4AT

Ⓑ **BARGAIN SALE!**

Top brand televisions and DVD players

20% off normal prices
Buy now – pay later
HURRY! Sale ends 15th July

Electromart

20 Summerton Road
Peckham

Ⓒ
Adults: Take 1 tablet with meals and at bedtime.
If your problem continues, seek medical advice. Do not give to children under 6 years of age.

Ⓓ **Best of Black Rainbow** (audio CD)

Our price £8.99   Save £4.99

20 of the band's hottest hits, including *I've seen it all before*, *Crash landing* and many more!

more info ▸   buy now ▸

b Read the sentences and write *T* (true), *F* (false) or *?* (the answer isn't in the text).

1 You mustn't enter the short story competition if you're older than eighteen. ☐
2 You don't have to write your short story before the end of October. ☐
3 Electromart is going to close on 15th July. ☐
4 Customers don't have to pay for a new TV or DVD player before they leave the shop. ☐
5 Adults have to take the tablets four times a day. ☐
6 Young children mustn't take these tablets. ☐
7 You usually have to pay £12 for *Best of Black Rainbow*. ☐
8 You have to get more information before you buy the CD. ☐
9 You don't have to pay for the CD with a credit card. ☐

5 Extension *New signs*

Use your imagination! In your notebook, draw two or three interesting new signs for your school. Write sentences explaining what they mean.

You mustn't bring penguins into the classroom.

1 Key vocabulary *Illness and injuries*

Read the sentences and complete the puzzle.

1	**F**						
2	**I**						
3	**R**						
4	**S**						
5	**T**						
6	**A**						
7	**I**						
8	**D**						

1 Mum's really scared of snakes. She nearly .... when she saw one in our garden!

2 Jack often feels .... if he travels by car. On a long journey we have to stop sometimes so that he can get out of the car.

3 Lisa's .... her arm and she can't move it at all. She fell when she was riding her horse on Sunday.

4 We all cheered and shouted at the concert. I came home with a .... throat!

5 Paul's .... his knee. It isn't a serious injury, but I don't think he'll be able to go surfing tomorrow.

6 Dad's worked in the garden all day and now he's got ....

7 The dentist worked on my teeth for nearly an hour. But he gave me an .... , so it didn't hurt.

8 The music was incredibly loud at the club. I've got a .... now.

2 should / shouldn't G➤ 16a

Complete the phone conversation between Jay and Ana. Use *should* or *shouldn't* with the verbs in the box.

work	feel	do
get	~~be~~	go	worry

JAY: How about going for a walk?

ANA: I can't, Jay. I have to work.

JAY: But it's a lovely afternoon.

You ¹*shouldn't be* inside on a day like this!

ANA: I know, but I've got my English exam next week.

JAY: You ² ....

Your English is excellent. You

³ .... confident about the exam.

ANA: Well, I don't feel confident. I feel tired.

JAY: That's because you're studying too much.

ANA: Well, what ⁴ .... I .... ?

JAY: You ⁵ .... all the time. You ⁶ .... lots of exercise and lots of fresh air. Exercise gives you energy.

ANA: So I ⁷ .... for a walk with you now, right?

JAY: Right.

3 Giving advice with should / shouldn't G➤ 16a, 16b

Read the problems and give advice. Write a sentence with *should* or *shouldn't* for each problem.

1 My girlfriend is angry because I forgot her birthday. What should I do?

You should ....

....

2 Our neighbours' dog has disappeared! What should they do?

....

....

3 My brother gets very bad headaches. What should he do?

....

....

4 I can never remember words in English. What should I do?

....

....

....

4 Listening

What's the problem?

a 🔲 Listen to five conversations about health problems. Match the people's names with the problems (a–g).

1 Adam ☐

2 Claire ☐

3 Emma ☐

4 Tom ☐

5 Sally ☐

---

a broken leg

b sore throat

c earache

d fainted

e headache

f toothache

g stomach ache

---

b 🔲 Listen again and write the names from 4a.

1 Who's had an accident recently?

   ----

2 Who was going to perform for a lot of people tonight?

   ----

3 Who eats too quickly?

   ----

4 Whose eyes were closed a few minutes ago?

   ----

5 Who's going to make a phone call?

   ----

5 Key expressions *Thanking people*

Complete the conversations. Choose from the list (a–h).

a very kind of you

b You're welcome.

c Thanks

d I'm

e That's

f Never mind.

g very much

h problem

A: You look really tired. I'll make you some tea.

B: ¹........ a lot.

A: ²........ OK. No ³........ .

A: Would you like to sit down?

B: Oh, that's ⁴........ . Thank you ⁵........ .

A: ⁶........ .

6 Extension *Odd one out*

Which is the odd one out? Give a reason for your answer.

1 injection (illness) medicine tablets

   The others are things that you get from a doctor.

2 sick fainted ill sore

   ----

3 earache stomach head knee

   ----

4 nurse dentist ambulance doctor

   ----

5 cold headache sore throat first-aid

   ----

6 broken hurt done move

   ----

7 mobile ring answer call

'Travel Smart': Vocabulary check

1 Look at the words in the box and find two adverbs.

Adverbs: ....

accidentally	custom	funeral	noisily
thumb	apologise	go away	lick
wedding	shake hands		

2 These sentences are wrong! ~~Cross out~~ the wrong word(s) and find the right word(s) in the box in Exercise 1.

1 French people usually ~~laugh~~ when they meet each other.

shake hands

2 A birthday is always a sad occasion.

....

3 I intelligently touched the door when my dad was painting it. He was really angry.

....

4 I was very sorry and I tried to sing to him, but he didn't want to listen. ....

5 In my village we always dance in the street on December 21st. It's an old crocodile.

....

6 Babies often put their leg in their mouth.

....

7 Jack, you've finished your soup. Don't wash your bowl. It isn't polite. ....

8 I don't want to talk to you. Please come here.

....

9 My cousin got married last Saturday and I went to the bathroom. ....

10 I couldn't go to sleep because my two little sisters were playing quietly in their bedroom.

....

3 Translate these sentences into your language.

1 We don't have to make a tomato sauce for the spaghetti. They sell ready-made sauces at the supermarket.

....

....

....

....

2 A: You look really ill. I'll call the doctor.
B: Thanks very much. That's very kind of you.

....

....

....

....

3 I must go now. I have to be at the station at eight o'clock. I mustn't miss my train.

....

....

....

4 Ow! I think I've broken my thumb.

....

....

5 If you eat too quickly, you'll get stomach ache. You should eat more slowly.

....

....

6 A: Harry, stop it! You shouldn't lick your plate like that. We're in a restaurant!
B: And you shouldn't speak so loudly. Everyone can hear you.

....

....

....

....

Unit 9 Learning diary

Date _____

Now I know how to:

	Easy	Not bad	Difficult
talk about obligations.	☐	☐	☐

At our school, students mustn't _____ .

At home I have to _____ .

	Easy	Not bad	Difficult
describe things that aren't necessary.	☐	☐	☐

My friend's lucky. He doesn't have to _____ .

Holidays are great. I don't have to _____ .

	Easy	Not bad	Difficult
give advice and say what is/isn't the right thing to do.	☐	☐	☐

Parents should _____ .

Parents shouldn't _____ .

	Easy	Not bad	Difficult
thank people.	☐	☐	☐

I'll help you. _____ *much.*

I'll give you $30.   That's _____ *you.*

	Easy	Not bad	Difficult
respond to thanks.	☐	☐	☐

Thanks. _____ *welcome.   Thank you.* _____ *problem.*

	Easy	Not bad	Difficult
write about customs in my country.	☐	☐	☐

KEY WORDS

Illnesses and injuries

I feel sick.	= _____ *(in my language)*
I had an injection.	= _____
She's broken her leg.	= _____
I've hurt my arm.	= _____
He's fainted.	= _____
He's got earache.	= _____
I've got a sore throat.	= _____
first-aid	= _____

WORD WORK

Adjective	Adverb
quick	*quickly*
angry	_____
careful	_____
bad	_____
anxious	_____
sad	_____
easy	_____
calm	_____

10 Where is it made?

1 Key vocabulary *Materials*

Complete the words for the materials.

1 Windows and bottles are made of ....   g.........................

2 Shoes, belts and bags are often made of ....   l.......................

3 .... is a good material for T-shirts and socks.   c.......................

4 Expensive spoons and forks are sometimes made of ....   s.......................

5 Bicycles and washing machines are made of ....   m.......................

6 Tables and shelves are often made of ....   w.......................

7 .... is a favourite material for wedding rings.   g.......................

8 '......... money' is another name for credit cards.   p.......................

2 Listening *At the market*

a Listen to the people (1–5) at the Portobello Road market. What are they talking about? Choose the right pictures and write the numbers 1–5 in the boxes.

b Listen again. Write the names of the materials under the pictures you chose in 2a.

A ☐

B ☐

C ☐

D ☐

----------------   ----------------   ----------------   ----------------

E ☐

F [1]

G ☐

H ☐

----------------   *leather*   ----------------   ----------------

3 Present simple passive (G) → 17a, 17b

Complete the sentences. Use the verbs in the present simple passive.

1 Baseball and American football .... in the USA. (*play*)

2 Gold .... for coins these days. (*not use*)

3 This rice .... from Thailand. (*import*)

4 Skyscrapers .... of wood. (*not make*)

5 About 6,800 languages .... in the world. (*speak*)

6 Cheese .... usually .... in China. (*not eat*)

7 A lot of the world's tea .... in India. (*grow*)

8 Wild kangaroos .... in Europe. (*not find*)

4 Present simple passive (G) → 17a

Look at the words. How many different sentences can you make in the present simple passive? Write your sentences in your notebook. Use *is, isn't, are* and *aren't*.

Books aren't sold in libraries.

English	made	all over the world.
Fiat cars	sold	gold.
Rice	made of	in libraries.
Books	spoken	in very cold countries.
The Golden Gate Bridge	grown	in Italy.

5 Key expressions *Expressing a reaction*

Write two possible replies for each conversation. Choose from the adjectives in the box.

| incredible great expensive awful |
| amazing crazy terrible cheap |
| interesting strange nice |

1 A: I got these three DVDs for £20 at the market.

   B: *That's great!* ....

   That's cheap! ....

2 A: I've just read that almost three billion cinema tickets are sold in India every year!

   B: ....

   ....

3 A: Matthew's got a fantastic leather jacket at home, but he never wears it.

   B: ....

   ....

4 A: Every minute, people destroy about 2,000 trees in the world's rainforests.

   B: ....

   ....

5 A: Australia's got lots of snakes, but there aren't any wild snakes in New Zealand.

   B: ....

   ....

6 Extension *Word circle*

How many irregular past participles can you make from the letters in the circle?

p s w
e t l a o
k d r b i
n e t

been, bitten, ...

....

....

....

1 Past simple passive (G) 17a, 17b

Complete the sentences. Use the past simple passive form of the verbs in the box.

not find	not watch	sell	build	not eat	~~discover~~	hold	steal

1 Gold *was discovered* in California in 1848.

2 The Egyptian pyramids .... probably .... between 2,700 and 2,500 BC.

3 Potatoes .... by Europeans before the 16th century.

4 Leonardo da Vinci's painting *Mona Lisa* .... from the Louvre Museum in 1911. It .... until 1913.

5 In 2000 a pair of red shoes .... for $600,000 in New York. They were Judy Garland's shoes in *The Wizard of Oz.*

6 The first World Cup .... in Uruguay in 1930. The matches .... by many people because television didn't exist at that time.

2 Present and past simple passive (G) 17a, 17b

Write the sentences in a different way. Use the verbs in the passive.

1 That factory doesn't make fridges.
   Fridges *aren't made in that factory* .

2 People eat curry with rice.
   Curry ....

3 They produced this leather in South America.
   This leather ....

4 Someone stole some DVD players.
   Some DVD players ....

5 They don't sell these magazines in Spain.
   These magazines ....

6 A lot of Canadians speak French.
   .... Canadians.

7 Shakespeare didn't write *Lord of the Rings*.
   .... Shakespeare.

8 The Americans didn't invent computers.
   .... the Americans.

3 Making questions

Complete the conversation between Melanie and her friend Judith. Write Judith's questions.

JUDITH: That's a new bag! [1] *When did you get it?*

MELANIE: I got it last week, when I was shopping with Liz.

JUDITH: It's really nice. [2] .... ?

MELANIE: It was made in Italy.

JUDITH: [3] .... leather?

MELANIE: Yes, it is.

JUDITH: I'd like to get one like that. [4] ....
.... ?

MELANIE: I bought it at the shop on the corner of Summer Street.

JUDITH: [5] .... ?

MELANIE: It was £32. You should go and have a look. They've got lots of nice bags in that shop.

JUDITH: Yes, that's a good idea. [6] ....
.... Saturday afternoon?

MELANIE: Yes, it is. It's open on Sunday morning too.

Read the article about Susan Dale. Then read the sentences and circle the right answer: a, b or c.

In 2003 Susan Dale started work at an animal sanctuary called Wildlife Protection. This sanctuary takes care of about 150 wild animals, including lions, tigers and leopards.

Susan got special training to work with these dangerous animals. Early every morning she gave them their food and during the day she took visitors round the sanctuary. After that, she cleaned the cages. This work was shared with six other people.

One of the cages belonged to Fariq, a six-year-old tiger. On 19th August Susan went in to clean his cage as usual. She was getting ready to leave when Fariq walked towards her. Susan wasn't scared, but she moved back towards the gate.

Then suddenly Fariq attacked. His long teeth sank into Susan's leg and he started to pull her backwards into the cage. She shouted and tried to open the tiger's mouth. She knew her life was in danger, but she didn't panic and after a few minutes she was able to escape.

Outside the cage, Susan was helped by other workers and an ambulance was called. Her leg was very badly injured and she lost a lot of blood. She was taken to hospital and had to stay there for several weeks.

Now Susan is walking again – and she really wants to get back to work. 'That might seem crazy, but I'm so happy when I'm with animals,' she says. She has never thought about leaving the sanctuary. For Susan, working with dangerous animals is the best job in the world.

1 The animal sanctuary
  a was opened in 2003.
  b is called Wildlife Protection.
  c has got 150 tigers.

2 After Susan got her job, she was
  a often nervous.
  b very tired.
  c specially trained.

3 The animals' cages weren't cleaned
  a every day.
  b early in the morning.
  c by Susan and the other workers.

4 The work at the sanctuary was done
  a by seven people.
  b by dangerous animals.
  c by visitors.

5 When Susan was attacked, she
  a was starting to clean Fariq's cage.
  b wasn't badly hurt.
  c was pulled backwards into the cage.

6 After she escaped, Susan
  a helped other workers.
  b got help from other people.
  c made a phone call to the hospital.

5 Extension *Time to talk*

a Frank is having a conversation with a friend. Read what he says.

FRANK:
• What's your favourite film?
• Oh yeah? I haven't seen that. What's it like?
• How many times have you seen it?
• What's it about?
• Who are the main characters?
• Was it made in America?
• Have you got it on DVD?

🔊 Now listen to the conversation.

b Read Frank's sentences again. Then imagine he's talking to you. Think about the answers you want to make.

c 🔊 Close your book, listen to the sentences and respond.

'The world of computer animation':
Vocabulary check

1 Look at the words in the box. Can you find a job and a part of the body?

software	realistic	engineer	emotion	script
muscle	introduce	computer-animated		

Job: ....   Part of the body: ....

2 Match the pictures with the words in the box in Exercise 1.

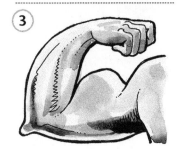

3 Translate these sentences into your language.

1 A: I like this little statue. Is it made of real gold?
   B: I don't think so. I think it's painted that colour.

----

2 These DVD players aren't made in Europe. They're imported from China.

----

3 A: In Britain seven billion plastic bags are used each year.
   B: That's amazing! I didn't know that.

----

4 A: When was this photo taken?
   B: It was taken when I was about nine.

----

5 Rabbits were introduced into Britain by the Romans.

----

6 A: Jack's in hospital. What happened?
   B: He was attacked by a dog in the park, but he wasn't badly injured.

Unit 10 Learning diary

Date _____

Now I know how to:

	Easy	Not bad	Difficult

- say what things are/were made of. ☐ ☐ ☐

  It isn't a real sword. It's _____ cardboard.

  Her necklace was _____ .

- say where things are/were produced. ☐ ☐ ☐

  These cars are _____ Japan.

  My DVD was _____ China.

- say who did something. ☐ ☐ ☐

  Dean didn't win. The race was _____ by an American.

  These photos _____ my grandfather.

- express a reaction. ☐ ☐ ☐

  This CD was only €2!   *Wow! _____ cheap!*

  Ella got 100% in all her exams.   *Really? _____ !*

- write a description of a film. ☐ ☐ ☐

KEY WORDS

Materials

cotton _____

_____

_____

_____

_____

_____

WORD WORK

Parts of speech

NOUN	ADJECTIVE	VERB	NOUN
success	*successful*	*paint*	*painting*
energy		*introduce*	

Talking

1 Key vocabulary *Relationships*

Read the sentences. Then put the numbers (1–7) in the right list.

GOOD RELATIONSHIPS	BAD RELATIONSHIPS
....	...*1*... ....

1 I have a row with my sister every day.
2 Sarah's very lucky because she gets on well with everyone.
3 I don't always agree with my friend Gary, but we never argue.

4 Annie annoys her parents because she's very unhelpful.
5 Paul and I have been close friends since we were at primary school.
6 We don't see each other very often, but we have a great time when we're together.
7 Liam spends too much time with his family and he always looks bored.

2 Reported speech 18a, 18b

Yesterday Pete phoned Kathy and asked her to go to the new sports centre with him.

Kathy and Pete are at the sports centre now. Look at the picture and complete Kathy's sentences. Use reported speech.

It's great. Everything's free. It stays open until eleven o'clock. We can have a game of tennis and we can have a swim too. There's an Olympic-size swimming pool. Then we can get something to eat at the café.

◄ 25 Metres ►

Café

CLOSED

Sports centre

Open 08.30 to 21.00

Entrance €8

1 Pete, you said (that) *it was great* ...., but it isn't very good.

2 You said ...., but we've just paid €8.

3 You said ...., but look, it closes at nine.

4 You said ...., but other people are using the tennis court.

5 You said ...., but the pool's only 25 metres.

6 You said ...., but it isn't open.

3 *say* and *tell* G→ 18c

Pete phoned Kathy again. Read their conversation and then rewrite the <u>underlined</u> sentences.
Use reported speech with *say* or *tell*.

PETE: Hi, Kathy. ¹<u>I'm going to the Ms Dynamite concert on Friday</u>. Do you want to come?

KATHY: No, ²<u>I'm staying at home on Friday</u>.

PETE: ³<u>I've got two tickets</u>. Why don't you come?

KATHY: No, thanks. ⁴<u>You can take someone else</u>.

PETE: But I bought the ticket for you. ⁵<u>I want to go with you</u>.

KATHY: ⁶<u>I don't want to go</u>.

PETE: ⁷<u>I know Ms Dynamite and we can meet her after the concert</u>.

KATHY: ⁸<u>I don't believe you</u>.

1 Pete *said* he <u>was going to the Ms Dynamite concert on Friday</u> .

2 Kathy *told* him she <u>was staying at home on Friday</u> .

3 He .... he ....

4 Kathy .... he ....

5 He .... her ....

6 She .... she ....

7 Pete .... that he .... and that ....

8 Kathy .... him ....

4 Reading *Curling*

Read the article by David Jones. Then read the sentences and write *T* (true), *F* (false) or *?* (the answer isn't in the text).

Have you ever tried curling?

by David Jones

I've just had my first curling lesson! Curling is one of Scotland's favourite winter sports. It is played on ice by two teams of four players. A rectangle 45 metres long and 4 metres wide is marked on the ice. At one end of the rectangle there is a circle.

The players have to send a large stone across the ice towards the circle. It weighs about 20 kg. The aim of the game is to get the stone as near the centre of the circle as possible. If team A's stones are nearer the centre than team B's, team A wins. The players use special brushes to sweep the ice in front of the stone, so that it goes more quickly. They wear special shoes and warm clothes.

It is very difficult to walk on the ice and I fell over several times before I even touched a stone! My teacher, Kay, told me that it was normal. 'Everyone thinks it's an easy sport,' she said.

'But professional players have to practise for years if they want to be really good.'

I was amazed when my first stone stopped next to the centre of the circle. Kay said it was beginner's luck! Then I fell over again ... and again. After half an hour on the ice, I was exhausted. Curling isn't easy. I think I'll just watch it on TV in future!

1 Curling is popular in Scotland.   *T*

2 In a curling match there are four players on the ice. ....

3 The players stand in the circle and send their stone across the ice. ....

4 Each player has two stones. ....

5 The players don't wear ordinary trainers. ....

6 David Jones isn't a professional player. ....

7 When David fell, Kay said she was amazed. ....

8 David doesn't think curling is easy. ....

5 Extension *What did they say?*

In your notebook, write three nice things that people have said to you. Use reported speech.

Adriana said she liked my new glasses.

1 Key expressions

Asking for clarification

Complete the conversation.
Choose the right sentences (a–i).

CARMEN: [1] *f*

RICHARD: She's quite tall and she's got long blond hair.

CARMEN: [2] ....

RICHARD: It means 'very fair', when you describe someone's hair.

CARMEN: Oh, I understand. It's *rubio* in Spanish. [3] ....

RICHARD: She's a university lecturer.

CARMEN: [4] ....

RICHARD: She's a university lecturer. She teaches at a university.

CARMEN: [5] .... So she's very intelligent.

RICHARD: Yes, she's really brainy.

CARMEN: Sorry, [6] ....

RICHARD: Brainy. She's got a big brain! I don't know the Spanish word.

CARMEN: I know. It's *listo*. 'Brainy.' Good, I've learnt two new words – *blond* and *brainy*.

a She's a university lecturer, isn't she?
b could you say that word again?
c What colour's her hair?
d Oh, I see.
e She's got blond hair, hasn't she?
f ~~What does your sister look like?~~
g What does 'blond' mean?
h What's her job?
i Pardon?

2 Question tags Ⓖ➔ 19a, 19b

Emily's outside a club. Complete the manager's sentences with question tags. Then write Emily's replies. Use the short answers in the box.

> No, I'm not.   ~~Yes, I do.~~   No, they can't.
> Yes, it does.   Yes, I am.

MANAGER: You want to come in, [1] *don't you* ?

EMILY: [2] *Yes, I do.*

MANAGER: The notice says 'Over 18 only', [3] .... ?

EMILY: [4] ....

MANAGER: People under 18 can't come in, [5] .... ?

EMILY: [6] ....

MANAGER: You aren't 18, [7] .... ?

EMILY: [8] ....

MANAGER: So you're too young, [9] .... ?

EMILY: [10] ....

3 Question tags Ⓖ➔ 19a

Complete the questions with question tags. Then guess what (or who) these people are talking about.

1 A: It isn't the African elephant, *is it* ?
   B: No, it's the blue whale.

   The largest animal in the world.

2 A: Shanghai's the capital, ... ?
   B: No, it's Beijing.

   ....

3 A: Abraham Lincoln was the first one, ... ?
   B: No, he wasn't. It was George Washington.

   ....

4 A: They don't live in the Arctic, ... ?
   B: No. You only find them in the Antarctic.

   ....

5 A: You've lost it, ... ?
   B: Yes. How can we get into the house?

   ....

6 A: You won, ... ?
   B: No, we didn't. We lost 1–0. They got a goal in the last minute.

   ....

4 Question tags Ⓖ▸ 19a

Imagine what these people are saying. Make sentences, using question tags.

①

A: It ....

.... ?

B: Yes, let's go back to the hotel.

②

A: You .... like ....

.... ?

B: Er, no, not really.

③

A: They ....

.... ?

B: Yes, I think so.

④

A: We ....

.... ?

B: No, we haven't.

5 Listening *Buying things on the telephone*

🔊 Claire's phoning a computer store in London.
She wants to buy a new computer game.
Listen to the conversation. Then answer the
questions. Circle a, b or c.

1 Where does Claire live?
   a In Manchester.
   b In London.
   c In Brighton.

2 What's Claire's surname?
   a Simmons
   b Simmonds
   c Simonds

3 What's the number of her house?
   a 7
   b 8
   c 3

4 What's Claire's postcode?
   a BN7 8FL
   b BM7 18FL
   c VN7 8FL

5 The man asks Claire to say two things again. What
   are they?
   a Her postcode and her address.
   b Her credit card number and her postcode.
   c Her postcode and her surname.

6 When will the shop send the CD Rom to Claire?
   a Next week.
   b Before the end of the week.
   c In a few weeks.

6 Extension *Think of some questions*

Write questions to go with these question tags.

*You can play DVDs on your computer,
can't you?*

1 ....

.... , can't you?

2 ....

.... , isn't it?

3 ....

.... , weren't they?

4 ....

.... , haven't you?

5 ....

.... , is she?

6 ....

.... , didn't she?

7 ....

.... , does he?

8 ....

.... , don't you?

'Wrong number': Vocabulary check

1 Look at the words in the box.
Find two words to express feelings.

....

be in	ring	be back	definitely
shocked	phone call	reply	
upset	wrong number		

2 Complete the sentences. Use words from the box in Exercise 1.

Hello, Paul!

1 I said hello to Paul, but he didn't

.... – he didn't even look at me.

2 Neil said he was going to call me yesterday, but

the phone didn't .... all day.

3 I'll .... see you tomorrow.

I promise.

4 Sarah's crying – she looks really

....

5 A: How long will you stay in London?

B: Only a week. I'll .... on

August 10th.

6 When the plane came down in the field near my

house, I couldn't believe it. I was really

....

7 I want to make a .... , but I can't

because I've left my mobile at home.

8 Will you .... this evening? I

want to come and see you.

9 A: Hello. Is that Kirsty?

B: No, this is 73628. I think you've got the

....

3 Translate these sentences into your language.

1 Jay said he got on well with his parents.

....

....

2 A: My phone number's 01456 823444.
   B: Pardon? Could you say that again?

....

....

....

3 A: How's Lizzie?
   B: She told me that she was feeling better.

....

....

....

4 A: I'll phone you at eight. You aren't going out this
     evening, are you?
   B: No, I'll definitely be in this evening.

....

....

....

5 A: What does 'brainy' mean?
   B: It means 'very clever'.

....

....

....

6 A: Fran isn't in a very good mood, is she?
   B: No. She's had a row with her boyfriend. They
     aren't talking to each other at the moment.

....

....

....

Unit 11 Learning diary

Date _____

Now I know how to:

	Easy	Not bad	Difficult

- report what people say. ☐ ☐ ☐

  ('I'm happy.') He said _____ .

  ('I can speak French.') She told _____ .

- use question tags to ask if something is true or not. ☐ ☐ ☐

  You're 15, _____ ?

  She's got a sister, _____ ?

- use question tags to ask if someone agrees. ☐ ☐ ☐

  It's cold today, _____ ?

  They didn't play well, _____ ?

- ask for clarification. ☐ ☐ ☐

  I don't know that word. What _____ it _____ ?

  Could _____ ? I didn't understand.

  P_____ ? I didn't hear what you said.

- write a conversation using the correct punctuation. ☐ ☐ ☐

KEY WORDS

Relationships

He annoys me.	=	_____ (in my language)
She's my closest friend.	=	_____
We had a row.	=	_____
We don't talk to each other.	=	_____
They argue a lot.	=	_____
I get on well with them.	=	_____
I spend a lot of time with him.	=	_____

WORD WORK

Verbs for 'speaking'

speak _____

answer _____

_____

_____

_____

_____

STEP1

1 Key vocabulary *American English*

Look at all the words in each sentence and decide if these people are speaking American English or British English. Then <u>underline</u> the right word in brackets.

1 When I was on (*vacation* / *holiday*), the lift at my hotel didn't work.

2 These (*trainers* / *sneakers*) will go well with my blue pants.

3 There were cookies all over the (*sidewalk* / *pavement*) and two dogs were eating them.

4 Your trainers are in the (*closet* / *wardrobe*).

5 I bought some biscuits at the local (*store* / *shop*).

6 You can buy sneakers on the third floor. The (*elevator* / *lift*) is over there.

7 Could you go to the store and get me some (*biscuits* / *cookies*)?

8 I'm going on vacation next week and I need some new summer (*trousers* / *pants*).

9 I can't take you to the clothes store because there isn't any (*gas* / *petrol*) in the car.

2 used to G⟶ 13a, 13b

Maggie is 16 now. She's remembering the time when she was very young. Complete the sentences using the right form of *used to*.

1 *I used to collect* .... (*I / collect*) photos of wild animals.

2 .... (*I / not like*) dogs.

3 .... (*I / not stay*) in bed late.

4 .... (*My brother and I / watch*) children's television every day.

5 .... (*We / never read*) magazines.

6 .... (*My mum / read*) a bedtime story to me every night.

3 used to *Questions* G⟶ 13a

Write a question about each of the sentences in Exercise 2.

1 What *did Maggie use to collect* .... ?

2 Did she ....
.... ?

3 Did she ....
.... ?

4 What .... they ....
.... ?

5 Did they ....
.... ?

6 What .... her mum ....
.... ?

4 Reading A teenage immigrant in the USA

a Read the article about Salim. Complete the text. Circle the right answer: a, b or c.

Salim ¹...... born in Guinea, West Africa. He came to America three years ago ²...... continue his education.

'Before I came, I ³...... watch American movies and I thought America was a wonderful place. I really wanted to go there. I remember the day I arrived. When I got ⁴...... the plane at the airport in New York, I went to the immigration desk. The man looked at my papers. My heart was beating fast. When he said OK, I couldn't believe it. I could ⁵...... in the USA!'

But at first, things weren't easy for Salim because he couldn't speak English.

'At school, I used to sit on my own because I ⁶...... communicate with anyone. In the park I used to play basketball on my own. The other kids used to throw stones at me, and they used to ⁷...... : "Go back to your own country." That was because they didn't know me and they didn't know anything about my culture.'

Salim can speak English now, but his life is still difficult. 'I go to school and I ⁸...... work as well. If I didn't work, I ⁹...... have enough money. I need money for myself and I ¹⁰...... money and clothes to my brothers and sisters in Guinea. I don't get ¹¹...... free time to have fun. Education is very important for me. I'm the first person in my family to go to college.'

Salim can't forget his home and his friends in Guinea and he often feels sad. The American way of life is very different from life in West Africa. But he's optimistic.

'I try to ¹²...... an American teenager. I've got baggy pants, sneakers, and I wear my baseball cap back to front. I listen to hip hop. I listen to *R&B, but I don't feel like an American teenager. But it's good here. Your dreams can come true if you work hard.'

*rhythm and blues – a style of music

1	a is	b has	c was
2	a and	b to	c for
3	a liked	b used to	c always
4	a off	b on	c into
5	a stay	b to stay	c stays
6	a couldn't	b could	c can't

7	a tell	b says	c say
8	a mustn't	b has to	c have to
9	a won't	b would	c wouldn't
10	a sent	b send	c sends
11	a many	b a lot	c much
12	a looks like	b look like	c like

b Answer the questions.

1 Where is Salim from?

   He's from Guinea in West Africa.

2 When he was in Guinea, where did he get his ideas about the USA?

   ....

3 How was he feeling when he got off the plane in New York?

   ....

4 At first, what was his biggest problem?

   ....

5 Who does Salim help?

   ....

6 He describes the clothes he wears. Why does he wear them?

   ....

5 Extension What did you use to do?

Imagine you're talking to the oldest person in your town. In your notebook, write at least three questions you'd like to ask him/her. Use the question form of used to.

Where did you use to live when you were a child? Did you ...? What ...?

1 Second conditional (G)→ 9

Complete the sentences.

1 If <u>I had</u> (I / have) more time, <u>I'd play</u> (I / play) computer games every evening.

2 If .... (I / can) meet someone from the past, ... (I / choose) Einstein.

3 If .... (my parents / not be) so stressed out, ... (we / not argue).

4 If .... (my hair / be) shorter, ... (I / look) nice?

5 If .... (I / go) to the USA, ... (I / go) to California.

6 If .... (you / have) a lot of money, what .... (you / do)?

7 If .... (I / not have) a mobile phone, ... (I / not able to) keep in touch with my friends.

2 What would they do? (G)→ 9

Write the sentences in a different way. Use the second conditional.

1 I want to buy a drink at the café, but I haven't got enough money, so I can't.

If I <u>had enough money, I'd buy a drink at the café.</u>

2 Natasha's boyfriend isn't at the party and she feels sad.

If her boyfriend ....

3 I want to take a lot of holiday souvenirs home, but my suitcase is too small, so I can't.

If my suitcase ....

....

4 I want to go surfing this afternoon, but I feel sick.

If I ....

5 I want to spend more time with my sister, but I don't get on well with her.

If I ....

....

6 My brother drinks eight cups of coffee a day and he gets bad headaches.

If my brother ....

....

7 People go everywhere by car because there aren't enough buses and trains.

If there ....

....

8 I want to have piano lessons but I haven't got enough time.

If I ....

3 Key expressions *Saying goodbye*

What would you say to these people?
Complete the sentences.

1 You've stayed at a friend's house for three days and now you're leaving.

   Thanks for having me. ....

2 You've just had a fabulous meal at a friend's house and now you're leaving.

   Thanks .... meal.

3 Your uncle's going home. He's getting on the train.

   .... journey.

4 You're leaving your friend's house after a party. You've really enjoyed it.

   Goodbye, Max. It was a fantastic party.

   .... time.

5 Your boyfriend/girlfriend is going away. You won't see him/her for three months.

   .... you.

6 Your friend's going to live abroad. You want to get lots of emails and text messages from him.

   .... in ....

4 Listening *Leaving Africa*

Molly, an English girl, has spent a month in a village in East Africa. She's saying goodbye to Duncan, a teacher at the village school. Listen to the dialogue and circle the right answer: a, b or c.

1 Today
   a Molly has just arrived in the village.
   b Molly's going back to England.
   c Molly's leaving London.

2 Molly
   a can stay for another month.
   b has decided to stay for another month.
   c would like to stay for another month.

3 During her month in the village
   a Molly has given Duncan English lessons.
   b Molly has given the children English lessons.
   c Molly wasn't a very good teacher.

4 Molly's flight is
   a at eight o'clock.
   b at three o'clock.
   c at half past one.

5 At the airport, Molly
   a is going to buy some presents for her family.
   b is going to send lots of emails.
   c won't have time to buy any souvenirs.

6 The children in the village
   a all speak English as a first language.
   b are learning English.
   c haven't enjoyed Molly's lessons.

5 Extension *Time to talk*

a It's the last day of the school term. Sally is having a conversation with a friend. Read what she says.

SALLY:
• Have you got any plans for the holidays?
• What else will you do?
• What would you do if you could choose?
• Are you going to get a holiday job?
• Right. We must keep in touch. What's your email address?

   Now listen to the conversation.

b Read Sally's sentences again. Then imagine she's talking to you. Think about the answers you want to make.

c Close your book, listen to the sentences and respond.

'That's amazing': Vocabulary check

1 Look at the words in the box. Can you find three verbs, two nouns, two adjectives and one adverb?

Verbs: ....

Nouns: ....

Adjectives: ....

Adverb: ....

grow	awake	stretch	contain	almost
main	traffic jam	cell		

2 Complete the sentences. Use the words in the box in Exercise 1.

1 English people love their gardens. They

.... lots of flowers and vegetables.

2 I'm sorry I'm late. There was a big ....

in town.

3 The ice caps of the Arctic and the Antarctic are

enormous. They .... 70% of the world's

fresh water.

4 The Andes go across South America. They

.... from Chile in the south to Venezuela

in the north.

5 This is a .... from the human body. It's so

small that we need a microscope to see it.

6 A: Are the children asleep?

B: No, they're .... , but they're still in bed.

7 I like doing a lot of things, but my ....

interests are music and sport.

8 I was in the USA for eleven and a half months –

.... a year.

3 Translate these sentences into your language.

1 A: I've had a great weekend. Thanks for having me.
  B: No problem. Have a good journey. And don't forget to keep in touch.

....

....

....

....

....

2 If you could travel at the speed of light, it would take eight minutes to get to the sun.

....

....

....

....

3 What hobbies did you use to have when you were young?

....

....

4 When I was little, I used to be afraid of dogs, and I didn't use to like thunder.

....

....

....

....

5 A: If you were a car, what car would you be?
  B: I wouldn't be an ordinary car. I'd be a Porsche GT.

....

....

....

....

6 Our school library contains over twenty thousand books.

....

....

Unit 12 Learning diary

Date _____

Now I know how to:

	Easy	Not bad	Difficult

- talk about things that happened regularly in the past. ☐ ☐ ☐

  When I was little, I used to _____ .

  I didn't use to _____ .

- say goodbye after a visit. ☐ ☐ ☐

  I've had a great week. Thanks for _____ me.

  I _____ miss you.

  Keep _____ . Write to me.

  Have _____ . I hope the train's on time.

- talk about imaginary situations. ☐ ☐ ☐

  If I had more money, I'd _____ .

  If I _____ , I'd _____ .

- write an essay about my country. ☐ ☐ ☐

KEY WORDS

American	British
gas	petrol
cookies	_____
_____	_____
_____	_____
_____	_____
_____	_____
_____	_____
_____	_____

WORD WORK

Synonyms

a <u>fantastic</u> film	wonderful
<u>more than</u> 20 people	_____
<u>approximately</u> ten years	_____
the <u>most important</u> thing	_____
I'm <u>almost</u> ready.	_____
They <u>make</u> computer chips.	_____
a <u>large</u> suitcase	_____
The match <u>begins</u> at 7.30.	_____

Grammar notes

Present simple

1a

AFFIRMATIVE AND NEGATIVE	
I/You/We/They	drink milk.
He/She/It	drinks milk.
I/You/We/They	don't drink milk.
He/She/It	doesn't drink milk.

QUESTIONS AND SHORT ANSWERS	
Do I/you/we/they	drink milk?
Does he/she/it	
Yes, I do. / No, she doesn't. (etc.)	

In the affirmative third person singular (*he/she/it*), we normally add *s* (*he drinks*). But:

– if a verb ends in *ch, sh, ss* or *o*, we add *es*.
  watch – he watch**es**   finish – it finish**es**
  cross – he cross**es**   go – she go**es**

– if a verb ends in a consonant (*b, c, d,* etc.) + *y*, we change the *y* to *ies*.
  try – he tr**ies**   carry – she carr**ies**

1b We use the present simple to talk about habits, regular activities and things that are generally true.

- Paul always **wears** a baseball cap.
- I **use** the Internet every day.
- A lot of people **don't like** snakes.
- **Does** Ana **live** in Veracruz?
- What **do** kangaroos **eat**?

Present continuous

2a

AFFIRMATIVE AND NEGATIVE	
I'm He's/She's/It's We're/You're/They're	dreaming.
I'm not He/She/It isn't We/You/They aren't	

QUESTIONS AND SHORT ANSWERS	
Am I Is he/she/it Are you/we/they	dreaming?
Yes, you are. / No, I'm not. Yes, she is. / No, they aren't. (etc.)	

2b We use the present continuous to talk about actions that are in progress now.

- I can't speak to you now. I'**m having** my lunch.
- Look! Sarah'**s crying**.
- What **are** those people **doing**?
- A: **Is** the film **starting**?
- B: Yes, it **is**. Hurry up.

2c Note the difference between the two present tenses.

- A: Look at Zoe. She'**s wearing** a long dress.
- B: Oh, yes. She usually **wears** jeans and a T-shirt.

2d We also use the present continuous to talk about arrangements for the future (see note 6).

Past simple

3a

AFFIRMATIVE AND NEGATIVE		
I/He/She/It/ We/You/They	started/ went	yesterday.
I/He/She/It/ We/You/They	didn't start / didn't go	

To form the past simple affirmative of regular verbs:

– we add *ed* to the infinitive.
  want – want**ed**   call – call**ed**

– with verbs ending in *e*, we add *d*.
  live – live**d**   arrive – arrive**d**

Irregular verbs have different forms in the past simple.

be – **was/were**   go – **went**   buy – **bought**

Look at the list of irregular verbs on page 142 in the Student's Book.

QUESTIONS AND SHORT ANSWERS	
Did I/he/she/it/ we/you/they	start yesterday?
Yes, I did. / No, we didn't. (etc.)	

3b We use the past simple to talk about past actions or situations.

- I **broke** my arm yesterday.
- Shreen **didn't speak** English when she **was** young. She only **spoke** Hindi.
- When **did** the Romans **come** to Britain?
- A: **Did** you **go** out last night?
- B: No, I **didn't**. I **stayed** at home.

Past continuous

4a

AFFIRMATIVE AND NEGATIVE	
I/He/She/It	was dreaming.
We/You/They	were dreaming.
I/He/She/It	wasn't dreaming.
We/You/They	weren't dreaming.

QUESTIONS AND SHORT ANSWERS	
Was I/he/she/it Were you/we/they	dreaming?
Yes, you were. / No, I wasn't. Yes, she was. / No, they weren't. (etc.)	

4b We use the past continuous to talk about actions or situations that were in progress in the past.

- There was a lot of noise. All the students **were talking**.
- We couldn't play tennis because it **was raining**.
- How many people **were waiting** for the bus?
- A: **Was** the driver **going** too fast?
- B: Yes, he **was**. That's why he had the accident.

4c We can use the past continuous and the past simple in the same sentence. One action was in progress (past continuous) when another action interrupted it (past simple).

- Sorry. I **was having** a bath when you **phoned**.
- I **was tidying** my room when I **found** this old photo.

The future: *will / won't*

5a

AFFIRMATIVE AND NEGATIVE	
I/He/She/It/ We/You/They	will ('ll) change.
I/He/She/It/ We/You/They	won't change.

QUESTIONS AND SHORT ANSWERS	
Will I/he/she/it/ we/you/they	change?
Yes, I will. / No, they won't. (etc.)	

5b We use *will/won't* + verb when we talk about future facts or predictions about the future.

- The sun **will rise** at 6.15 tomorrow.
- I**'ll be** seventeen next Thursday.
- A: I've got some mushroom soup for lunch. **Will** Fiona **like** it?
- B: No, she **won't**. She **won't eat** it. She hates mushrooms.

5c We use *will/won't* when we decide to do something at the moment of speaking. This is sometimes an offer or a promise.

- Who can I ask? I know! I**'ll phone** Alice.
- Are you too hot? I**'ll open** a window.
- I**'ll buy** some bread. I **won't forget**, I promise.

5d Note the position of *probably* with *will* and *won't*.

- The shops **will probably** be closed now.
- I **probably won't** see you tomorrow.

5e We generally use *will/won't be able to* as the future form of *can/can't*.

- If you sit there, you **won't be able to** see the screen.
- A: I can't do my maths homework.
- B: Ask Jack. He**'ll be able to** help you.

The future: present continuous

6 We use the present continuous to talk about definite arrangements for the future, things that are already organised.

- A: What **are** you **doing** tonight?
- B: I**'m staying** at home. My uncle**'s coming** for dinner.

The future: *going to*

7 We use *am/is/are* + *going to* + verb to talk about intentions for the future. We have decided to do something before we speak.

- A: **Are** you **going to sell** your bike?
  B: Yes, I'm **going to get** a new one.
- I'm **not going to argue** with my sister. That's my New Year's resolution!

First conditional

8 We use *if* + present simple + *will* (*'ll*)/*won't* + verb when we talk about a possible future action or situation and its result.

- **If** the weather **improves**, we'**ll go** to the beach. (NOT *If the weather will improve*)
- **If** the bus **doesn't come** soon, we'**ll be** late for school.
- You **won't look** nice **if** you **wear** those old trousers.
- What **will** you **do** if the shops **aren't** open?

Second conditional

9 We use *if* + past simple + *would*(*'d*)/*wouldn't* + verb when we imagine a present or future situation that isn't very probable.

- If I **saw** a ghost, I'**d be** terrified.
  (= But I probably won't see a ghost.)
- If you **didn't spend** hours on your computer, you **wouldn't have** a headache.
  (= But you spend hours on your computer, and the situation probably won't change.)
- What **would** you **do** if you **won** £1,000,000?

might

10 We use *might/might not* + verb to say that something is possible but not certain. It can refer to the present or the future.

- A: Where's Laura?
  B: I'm not sure. She **might be** at the sports centre.
- I don't feel very well, so I **might not go out** tonight.

Present perfect

11a

AFFIRMATIVE AND NEGATIVE		
I/We/You/They	have ('ve)	improved.
He/She/It	has ('s)	changed.
I/We/You/They	haven't	
He/She/It	hasn't	

QUESTIONS AND SHORT ANSWERS	
Have I/we/you/they	changed?
Has he/she/it	
Yes, I have. / No, she hasn't. (etc.)	

We form the present perfect with *have/has* + the past participle of the main verb.

The past participle ending is *ed* for regular verbs. Irregular verbs have different forms for the past participle.

Look at the list of irregular verbs on page 142 in the Student's Book.

11b We use the present perfect to describe the present result of a past action.

- Look. I'**ve bought** a new mobile.
  (Past action: *I bought it.*
  Present result: *I've got it NOW.*)
- I **haven't finished** my lunch.
- Why **has** the clock **stopped**?
- A: **Have** you **seen** my bag?
  B: No, I **haven't**.

11c We often use *never* with the present perfect. *Never* means *not up to now*.

- I'**ve never travelled** by plane.

We use the question form of the present perfect with *ever* to ask about people's experiences. *Ever* means *up to now*.

- **Have** you **ever travelled** by plane?
- **Has** a member of your family **ever won** a competition?

11d We use the present perfect with *just* to say that something happened a very short time ago.

- A: Your hair's wet.
  B: I know. I'**ve just washed** it.

11e We use the present perfect with *for* and *since* to talk about a present situation.

We use *for* to show how long something has continued.

for a fortnight, for ages, for two weeks, (etc.)

- A: *How long have you had your camera?*
  B: *I've had it for a long time. It's very old.*

We use *since* to say when something began.

since 2001, since last Saturday, since my birthday, (etc.)

- *I haven't seen Fran since the day before yesterday.*

11f Note the use of the past participle *been*.

- *My father has been a teacher for 20 years.*
  (been = the past participle of the verb *be*)
- *I've been to the USA three times.*
  (been = the past participle of the verb *go*)

Present perfect and past simple

12 Note the difference between the present perfect and the past simple.

- *Look. I've broken my watch.*
  (Present perfect: past action + present situation)

We don't say when the action happened.

- *I broke my watch at school yesterday.*
  (Past simple: past action)

We often say when the action happened (*yesterday*) or we give more details (*at school*).

used to

13a

AFFIRMATIVE AND NEGATIVE	
I/He/She/It/ We/You/They	used to drink milk.
I/He/She/It/ We/You/They	didn't use to drink milk.

QUESTIONS AND SHORT ANSWERS	
Did I/he/she/it/ we/you/they	use to annoy everybody?
No, I didn't. / Yes, they did. (etc.)	

13b We use *used to* + verb to talk about activities or situations that happened regularly in the past. Often, these things don't happen now.

- *When I was little I used to spend hours on my own. I didn't use to play with other children.*
- A: *Did you use to have a bedtime story?*
  B: *Yes, I did.*
- A: *I came to live here last week.*
  B: *Where did you use to live?*

must / have to

14

AFFIRMATIVE		
I/We/You/They	must have to	stop.
He/She/It	must has to	

Note that *must* is followed by the infinitive without *to*. We use *must* and *have to* to talk about obligation.

Must and *have to* sometimes mean the same.

- *It's very cold. You must wear / have to wear your coat!*
- *There's too much noise. It must stop / has to stop immediately!*

But we normally use *must* when the speaker is expressing a personal opinion.

- *I've got toothache. I must go to the dentist.*

And we normally use *have to* when the obligation comes from a rule or an arrangement.

- *I have to go to the dentist at 2.30.*

mustn't / don't have to

15

NEGATIVE		
I/We/You/They	don't have to	
He/She/It	doesn't have to	start at 7.30.
I/He/She/It/ We/You/They	mustn't	

We use *mustn't* to describe an obligation (for example, to give an order). There isn't a choice.

We use *don't have to* to say that something isn't necessary. There is a choice.

- *You mustn't walk home. It's after midnight.*
  (= Don't walk home!)
- *You don't have to walk home. You can get a bus.*
  (= You can walk home if you like, but it isn't necessary.)

should / shouldn't

16a

AFFIRMATIVE AND NEGATIVE	
I/He/She/It/ We/You/They	should eat that.
I/He/She/It/ We/You/They	shouldn't eat that.

QUESTIONS AND SHORT ANSWERS	
Should I/he/she/it/ we/you/they	eat that?
Yes, I should. / No, they shouldn't. (etc.)	

16b Note that *should/shouldn't* are followed by the infinitive without *to*.

We use *should/shouldn't* when we give or ask for advice and when we think something is/isn't the right thing to do.

- You **shouldn't use** your computer during a storm. You **should turn** it **off**.
- We **should** always **try** to help other people.
- A: What **should** I **do**? **Should** I **apologise**?
  B: Yes, you **should**.

The passive: present and past

17a

	be	Past participle	
Tea	is	imported	from India.
This car	isn't	made	in England.
Penguins	are	found	in the Antarctic.
They	aren't	found	in the Arctic.
I	was	invited	to Ella's party.
The driver	wasn't	hurt	in the accident.
These photos	were	taken	in 1920.
Things	weren't	made	of plastic in 1900.

We form the passive with *be* + the past participle of the main verb.

17b We use the passive when we want to talk about the action and when it isn't important to say who does/did the action.

- The house **was built** in 1980. [Passive]
  (Here we're interested in the date. We aren't interested in the people who built the house.)
- My grandfather **built** the house in 1980. [Active]
  (Here we're interested in the person who built the house as well as the date.)

We can use *by* in a passive sentence to say who does/did the action.

- A: *Who uses the computer?*
  B: *It's **used by** all the family.*

Reported speech

18a In reported speech we often change the present tense to the past tense.

Direct speech	Reported speech
PRESENT SIMPLE 'Kate **annoys** me.'	PAST SIMPLE He said (that) Kate **annoyed** him.
'I **don't eat** fish.'	She said she **didn't eat** fish.
AM/IS/ARE 'We**'re** hungry.'	WAS/WERE They said they **were** hungry.
'I**'m** not lazy.'	She said she **wasn't** lazy.
HAS/HAVE GOT 'I**'ve got** a cold.'	HAD She said she **had** a cold.
'I **haven't got** a job.'	He said he **didn't have** a job.
CAN 'Jack **can** come.'	COULD She said Jack **could** come.
'I **can't** dance.'	He said he **couldn't** dance.

18b We can often leave out *that* before a reported statement.

- *Mum said **that** I could go out tonight.*
  OR *Mum said I could go out tonight.*

18c We use *say* and *tell* to introduce reported speech.

We use *tell* when we mention the person we're speaking to.

We use *say* when we don't mention the person we're speaking to.

- *Sarah **told me** she had a new boyfriend.*
- *Sarah **said** she had a new boyfriend.*
  (NOT Sarah said me she had a new boyfriend.)
- *I **told my dad** that I wanted a new bike.*
- *I **said** I wanted a new bike.*

Question tags

19a

Affirmative	Negative tag
I'm right,	**aren't** I?
He's 16,	**isn't** he?
We've got time,	**haven't** we?
Zoe's finished,	**hasn't** she?
They **can** win,	**can't** they?
You'll help me,	**won't** you?
She **likes** eggs,	**doesn't** she?
He **went** home,	**didn't** he?

Negative	Affirmative tag
I'm **not** late,	**am** I?
She **isn't** here,	**is** she?
We **haven't** got any salt,	**have** we?
Jay **hasn't** phoned,	**has** he?
They **can't** swim,	**can** they?
You **won't** forget,	**will** you?
They **don't** speak French,	**do** they?
He **didn't** eat his lunch,	**did** he?

We use a negative tag after an affirmative statement, and an affirmative tag after a negative statement.

– After *be, have, can* and *will*, we use the same verb in the question tag.

– After a verb in the present simple (*She likes / They don't speak*), we use *do/does* or *don't/doesn't* in the question tag.

– After a verb in the past simple (*He went / He didn't eat*), we use *did* or *didn't* in the question tag.

19b We use question tags to ask:

'Is this true?'
- *Holly's got a DVD player, **hasn't she**?*

'Do you agree?'
- *The weather's awful, **isn't it**?*

What's ... like?/What does ... look like?

20a We use *What's he/she/it like?* or *What are they like?* to ask for a description of someone/something.

- A: **What's** your sister **like**?
  B: *She's very friendly and she's a good dancer.*
- A: **What was** the film **like**?
  B: *It was very exciting and a bit scary.*

20b We use *What + do/does /did + look like?* to ask about the appearance of a person or thing.

- A: **What does** your new boyfriend **look like**?
  B: *He's quite tall and he's got dark hair.*
- A: **What did** the fish **look like**?
  B: *They were grey and white.*

turn on/off, plug in, take out, put in

21 These 'two-word' verbs are called *phrasal verbs*. Note the word order. When the object is a noun, there are two possibilities.

- *Turn the television **off**!*
  *OR Turn **off** the television!*
- *The oven's hot now. You can put the potatoes **in**.*
  *OR You can put **in** the potatoes.*

But when the object is a pronoun (*it, them,* etc.) only one word order is possible.

- *Did you hear me? Turn **it off**! (NOT Turn off it!)*
- *OK. I'll put **them in** for about twenty minutes.*

Suggestions

22a We use a question word + *shall we* + verb to ask other people for suggestions.

- *What **shall we** do?   Where **shall we** go?*
- *What time **shall we** meet?   Who **shall we** invite?*

22b Note the different ways of making suggestions.

- **Shall we** *play cards?*
- **Why don't we** *go to the park?*
- **Let's** *meet at ten o'clock at the station.*
- **How about** *inviting everybody in the class?*

Remember that we use the *-ing* form of the verb after *How about*.

a lot of /lots of, much and many

23a We use *a lot of* or *lots of*

– with countable nouns to describe a large number.

- *A lot of / Lots of people came to the concert.*

– with uncountable nouns to describe a large amount.

- *There's a lot of / lots of cheese in the fridge.*

We generally use *a lot of* / *lots of* in affirmative sentences. But we can use them in negative sentences and questions too.

- *I'm going sailing, but there isn't **a lot of** wind.*
- *Have you got **lots of** friends?*

23b We use *much* with uncountable nouns to describe an amount of something.

- *How **much** pasta do you want?*
- *That's good. There isn't **much** traffic this morning.*

We use *many* with plural nouns to describe a number of things or people.

- *Do you know **many** English people?*
- *The town isn't very interesting. There aren't **many** places to visit.*

We generally use *much* and *many* in questions and negative sentences. But we sometimes use *many* in affirmative sentences.

- ***Many** people think that tennis is a boring game.*

too much, too many and enough

24a We use *too much* with uncountable nouns (*salt, noise, money*, etc.).

- *Ugh! This soup is awful. There's **too much** salt.*

We use *too many* with countable nouns (*tourists, cars, people*, etc.).

- *I don't go to that beach in summer. There are **too many** tourists.*

24b We use *enough* with countable and uncountable nouns.

- *Have you got **enough** bread, or do you want another piece?*
- A: *There are 20 students in the class.*
  B: *We haven't got **enough** books. We've only got 15.*

Comparatives and superlatives

25a For adjectives with one syllable, we add *er* or *r* for the comparative, and *the* + *est* or *st* for the superlative.

- (old) *My sister's **older** than me.*
- (nice) *I think Jack's **the nicest** person in the class.*

When the adjective ends in 1 vowel + 1 consonant, we double the consonant in the comparative and the superlative.

*big – **bigger**/**the biggest***

*hot – **hotter**/**the hottest***

25b For most adjectives with two or more syllables, we use *more* and *the most* to form the comparative and the superlative.

- *Your mobile's **more modern** than mine.*
- *Happiness is **more important** than money.*

25c For two-syllable adjectives ending in consonant + *y*, we use *ier*/*iest* for the comparative and the superlative.

- (tidy) *Your room's **tidier** than mine.*
- (happy) *My dad is **the happiest** person I know.*

25d Note these irregular comparative and superlative forms.

- (good) *The weather's awful at the moment. Perhaps it'll be **better** this afternoon. Who's **the best** football player in the world?*
- (bad) *I don't like going in the car with my dad. He's a **worse** driver than my mum. I hate Mondays. I think Monday is **the worst** day of the week.*

as ... as ...

26 We use *as* + adjective + *as* to say that two things or people are the same, and *not as* + adjective + *as* to say they're different.

- *The blue whale's tongue is **as heavy as** an African elephant.*
- *The bus to London isn't **as fast as** the train, but it isn't **as expensive**.*
- *Your brother's a brilliant tennis player. Are you **as good as** him?*